Invoice Verification for SAP R/3

Stephen Birchall

MW01100948

Contents

Contents

Preface

There are many organizations that have implemented SAP and suffered from problems and confusion relating to the invoice verification functionality. Many of the implementations I have seen get it very wrong and the result is a function that is seen as inefficient, complex and time consuming. This does not have to be the case. If you spend time understanding exactly what the SAP functionality is trying to achieve and how to use the standard functionality to the fullest, you will reduce the risk of problems and find that the functionality is better than it appears to be initially.

This book begins by explaining the basic process in a non-technical manner. Other chapters focus on the functionality in detail and show how to configure each option to obtain the maximum benefits. It shows the many useful features available that are often overlooked and it explains some common misconceptions about certain options that are available and guides you to the correct choices.

Whether you are about to implement the invoice verification function, or you have already done so, you will find this book informative, even if you don't believe you are having any problems with the functionality.

Acknowledgments

This book is dedicated to my grandchildren: Stephen, Harvey, Rupinder, Balvinder, George, and one more who's on the way. To my precious wife Joan, and to all of our children, who constantly make me so glad to be a part of their lives. And to all of my colleagues, who have endured my terrible sense of humor. I would also like to thank my editor, Jawahara Saidullah, for the help and occasional crack of the whip that helped me complete the book.

1 What is Invoice Verification?

Invoice verification allows you to capture the details of vendor invoices. If the details of an invoice match the expected details that are specified by any related purchase order and goods receipts, the invoice can be automatically made available for payment. Unmatched invoices are excluded from the payment run and need to be investigated and released before payments can be made. If this process is overly complex or conducted inefficiently, payments made to vendors will be late. Possible consequences of this include a loss of cash discounts and even losing the vendor account and having purchase orders rejected by the vendor.

It is essential, therefore, to understand the basic process of invoice verification before you design or modify it. The standard process provided by SAP is very likely suitable for most businesses, though this may not appear to be the case at first. The standard process has many configuration options and is normally more than flexible enough to cater to the needs of an invoice-verification department. You are most likely to succeed if you adopt the standard SAP process, rather than trying to alter the SAP process to fit your current functionality. Most problems are caused by a misunderstanding of the standard SAP Invoice Verification process, and this leads to a design that is a compromise. So we will start with a high-level view of the process.

1.1 High-Level Process

The main aim of any invoice-verification process is to ensure that vendors are paid the correct amount at the right time (not too late but also not too early). The process should have a high incidence of first-time matching, to ensure that as little time as possible is spent trying to manually match invoices that appear to be incorrect. It is

important to include as few steps as possible in the process, considering that the process of handling payments does not in itself add value to the company or to the vendor.

The Main Steps

The main steps included in the process are:
- The capture of the vendor's invoice details
- The matching of those details to the details that we believe to be correct
- The investigation of any mismatches
- The release for payment of matched invoices
- The accounting entries involved (including taxes and delivery costs)
- The details recorded for audit purposes

It is important to keep these steps to a minimum and the SAP processes do achieve this. Additional steps are counter-productive and add little or no additional value.

Capture and matching occur in one transaction (transaction MIRO). This also includes the automatic release for payment if the match is successful. Figure 1.1 shows the main screen of the MIRO transaction.

The handling of mismatched invoices occurs in transaction MRBR, which also includes the release for payment if the invoice is successfully matched. Figure 1.2 shows the main selection screen of the MRBR transaction

The accounting entries are updated when the values are posted (in both transactions), as are the records of events for audit or inquiry purposes. Effectively these two transactions are the main steps involved. The only other transactions needed to manage the process are inquiry or cancellation transactions. If you have built your process to include more steps than this, you may be adding extra complexity for little or no extra value.

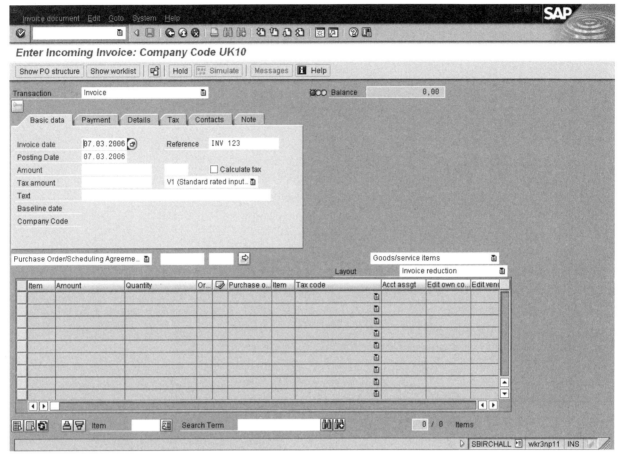

Figure 1.1 Main MIRO Transaction Screen

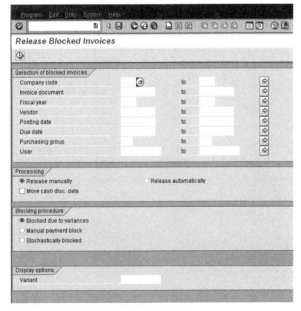

Figure 1.2 Main MRBR Transaction Selection Screen

Capturing the Invoice Details

This step uses transaction MIRO and is the main step in the process. If the details on the invoice match the details of what we believe to be owed to the vendor, then this transaction completes the process and passes the details to the payment run to ensure that the vendor is paid at the correct time. No further steps are required if the invoice matches here. While this is an important transaction, it does not need to be carried out only by senior financial staff. This is a common misconception.

The Use of Invoice Verification

This transaction is designed to be used by any member of the financial staff, however junior that person may be. The reason for this becomes clear when you see exactly what this transaction is doing. Its main purpose is simply to capture the details from the invoice sent in by the vendor, even though it appears to do much more than this.

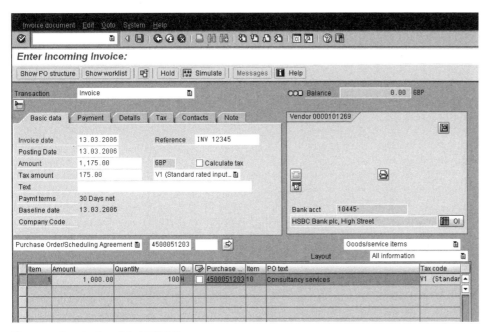

Figure 1.3 Sample Completed MIRO Screen

Figure 1.3 shows the MIRO main screen with the details completed.

The system will then use those details to attempt a match against what we believe the vendor is entitled to; only if this matches will a payment be proposed. Figure 1.4 shows the traffic light icon and zero balance that indicate that the invoice match is successful.

Figure 1.4 Traffic-Light Icon and Zero-Balance Indicating Successful Invoice Match

Some people assume that selected finance staff should use this transaction only because the operator can change details on the screen to match the details on the vendor's invoice. This occurs when the operator is entering the details and the vendor is asking for more (or less) than the amount we believe is due. But if you remember that this transaction is really just capturing the details from the invoice, then you realize that changing the details is not actually authorizing any payment. In fact, this transaction doesn't even require human input; it can be carried out using scanning equipment and appropriate software (in fact several organizations already use this method to enter invoices into SAP). So you must think of this pro-

cess as a method of capturing the invoice details, with the rest happening automatically. If the invoice matches, then it is passed for payment. If it does not match, the details are still captured but the payment is blocked.

Processing Mismatched Invoices

The standard way of managing mismatched or blocked invoices in SAP is to use transaction MRBR. Mismatched invoices are those where the details on the invoice do not match the details expected according to the purchase order. This transaction lists all of the invoices that have been blocked for payment. It gives full details of what is blocked, what value is involved, why it has been blocked, when, and by whom. Figure 1.5 shows a typical list of mismatched invoices displayed using transaction MRBR.

If investigation shows the vendor's details were correct, then the details of the purchase order or goods receipt should be corrected so that the invoice details match. MRBR will automatically release that invoice for payment once the reasons for the block are no longer valid, but only if you schedule MRBR as a regular job to release all invoices that no longer mismatch.

If the blocks are still valid—that is, if we disagree with the vendor's details—then the invoice can remain blocked for as long as required, or until a credit note has been posted. If, in certain unusual circumstances, the

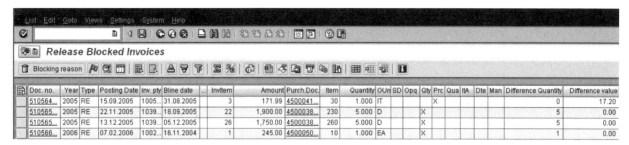

Figure 1.5 MRBR List Screen Showing Mismatched Invoices

vendor's invoice details are correct but we cannot change the purchase order or goods receipt details to ensure a match, we can use MRBR to remove blocks manually and release invoices even though they do not match. For this reason, MRBR is a transaction that must be limited to selected people in the business. These must be people with authority to write a company check, as they are effectively paying a vendor for something that we have indicated that we do not owe them for.

1.2   Handling Mismatched Invoices

There are two main situations in which you have to deal with mismatched invoices. These are:

▶ During input (in MIRO)
▶ After the input of the invoice

Mismatches During Input (MIRO)

The MIRO transaction performs two main checks:

▶ The first ensures that the details entered add up mathematically.
▶ The second checks to see if the invoice should be blocked or made available for payment.

The second check relies on the majority of the configurable invoice tolerances. After all, a mathematical check is not meant to deliver approximate results. Having said this, there is one tolerance that relates to the first check, and is known as the *manage-small-differences tolerance*. This is designed to control the allowed rounding errors (mainly during tax calculations). So, if the documents mathematically match within the configured tolerance, the system can then accept this as a rounding error and allow the process to continue to the next stage, where the remainder of the invoice tolerances can be checked.

When posting an invoice, the system will fill in most of the data for you. The data normally is taken from the purchase order referenced in the purchase order field on the main screen of transaction MIRO, and so this may not match the actual details from the invoice. This means that when the system adds up the line items and compares the result against the total value you entered in the **Amount** field of the basic data tab, it will not add up mathematically.

To post the invoice, you must make sure that the value of the line items adds up to the **Amount** field value (with taxes considered). This means that you will have to change the quantities and values that the system has proposed in order to match the quantities and values specified on the vendor's invoice. Figure 1.6 shows the MIRO main screen with the **Amount** field entered and the line details proposed by the system, based on data taken from the referenced purchase order.

This is where some people mistakenly get the idea that changing these values is somehow authorizing the payment. In reality, it is simply ensuring that the system knows the details of the invoice so that a match can be attempted. Think of it this way: If the system did not try to help by filling in the expected quantities and values, then you would have to enter them manually every time. All that is happening is that the system is trying to save time for you by filling in what it thinks the invoice should contain. So changing these values is not authorizing payment, merely indicating what the vendor is asking for.

The second check is where the main tolerances play a part. If the differences are within the tolerances, then the invoice is posted and the payment is not blocked.

If the differences are outside the tolerances, then the invoice is still posted but the payment is blocked. So tolerances really only control whether the payment is to be blocked; they do not control whether the invoice can be posted (apart from the rounding tolerance, i.e. small differences). Figure 1.7 shows an invoice that does not balance mathematically. The invoice total is 2,350 and the VAT is 350, but the value from the purchase order (price multiplied by un-invoiced receipts) does not add up to this value. Therefore, the invoice cannot be posted because of this mathematical discrepancy.

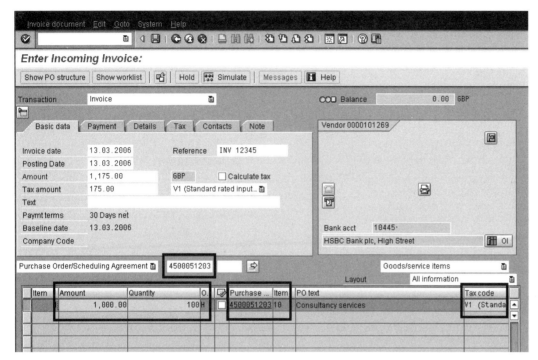

Figure 1.6 MIRO Screen Showing Data Obtained from Referenced Purchase Order

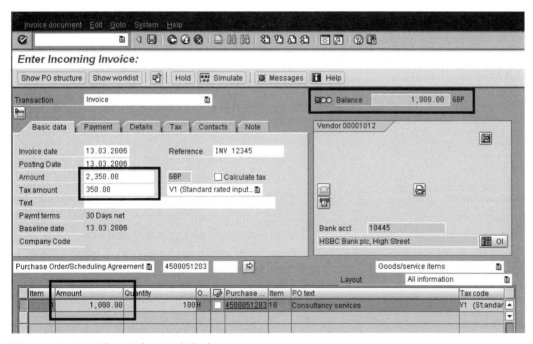

Figure 1.7 Invoice Failing Mathematical Check

1.3   Processing Blocked Invoices

When an invoice has been blocked for payment due to a mismatch that is outside the invoice tolerances, all that is different from an invoice that has not been blocked for payment is the setting of the payment blocking flags. Figure 1.8 shows an invoice with a payment-blocking flag (In this case an **R** to indicate an invoice-verification block). The financial postings are the same. The value is still shown as an open item on the vendor account, so any effect on the moving average price (or price variance account) will still occur, even if the document is blocked. The only action that is required to process blocked invoices is to decide if the blocks should be removed. There are two ways to remove the blocks, both using transaction MRBR These are:

▶ Manually, by indicating which block or blocks are to be removed

▶ Automatically, by running MRBR with the automatic release flag set on

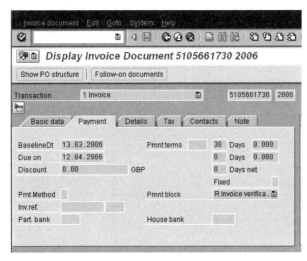

Figure 1.8 Payment-Blocking Flag

Many people make the mistake of simply removing the blocks using a financial transaction such as FBL1N. This removes the flag and allows a payment to be made, but it does not process the blocked record properly, so the items still appear in the blocked invoice transaction (MRBR) even after they have been released. Figure 1.9 shows the FBL1N screen that should not be used to manually release invoices.

Caution: Only use MRBR to process blocked invoices, to avoid corrupting the data used by MRBR.

Using Workflow when Mismatches Occur

Someone will have to investigate when an invoice is blocked during MIRO, but how are they informed that there is a problem and what caused it? Many organizations simply photocopy the invoice and pass it to the appropriate department with a handwritten explanation of the problem. This works well enough if the volumes of invoices that are posted are low and only a few people are involved in the investigations. This keeps it simple and is often the best way.

However, if the volumes are large and/or many people are involved in the investigations, then a more sophisticated solution is required. This is where workflow plays a very useful part in the process. MIRO can trigger a workflow message (normally an SAPmail or email message that can be formatted to suit your needs) to an appropriate user whenever a mismatch occurs. This is normally a request to correct a price or complete a goods receipt to make the details match the invoice.

The usual response to these messages is to carry out the change or to reply stating that the details are correct and the vendor's invoice should not be paid. This is a standard option in SAP and requires minimal configuration and setup, ideally with the help of your workflow consultant.

Using MRBR

MRBR should be checked regularly, and this transaction should be seen as the sole transaction for managing the release of blocked invoices. You can list blocked invoices by vendor, by date, by purchasing group, or by user, among other criteria. The system will then display the blocked invoices that match the selection options, and you will then be able to release invoices manually. Figure 1.10 shows an example of the screen used to manually manage blocked invoices.

This should only be necessary when you do not wish to change the purchase order to correct the price or when you wish to pay for the items even though a receipt may not be have been fully posted. To release an invoice, you can either select individual blocking reasons (quantity,

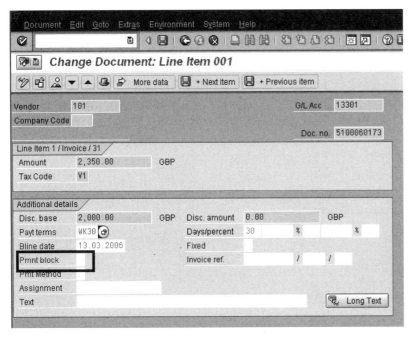

Figure 1.9 Initial FBL1N Transaction Screen

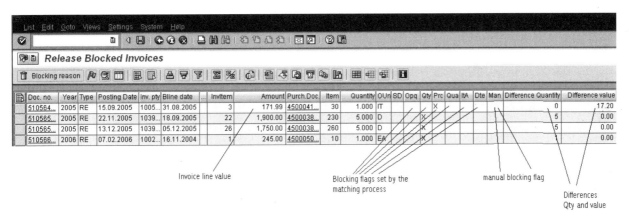

Invoice line value

Blocking flags set by the
matching process

manual blocking flag

Differences
Qty and value

Figure 1.10 Mismatched Invoices Displayed Within Transaction MRBR

price, date, etc.) and remove the block, or simply release the whole invoice.

Note: You cannot release part of an invoice for payment. The invoice is either blocked or available for payment in total.

Automatic invoice release

There is actually no setting for automatic invoice release for payment as such. If you have an invoice that is blocked

because the goods receipt has not yet been posted and then the goods receipt is posted, the invoice will not be automatically released for payment. However you can use transaction MRBR in a scheduled job with the flag **Release automatically** set on, and this will then release all invoices where the blocking reason is no longer relevant. This will then act the same as an automatic release, but will only release when the job has run. Ideally, this should be at least once a day. Figure 1.11 shows the position of the flag on the initial screen of transaction MRBR.

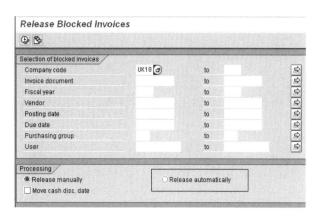

Figure 1.11 *Release Automatically* Flag in MRBR Initial Screen

1.4   Parking Invoices

The Invoice Parking functionality provided by SAP has a very specific purpose, and if you are using it for this purpose then it functions well. If, on the other hand, you are using the parking process as a specific step in the normal processing of invoices, then you may find that it is not designed for this purpose and you may experience problems.

The function has been provided to address situations where, for whatever reason, the user does not wish to complete the invoice-verification transaction but wishes to keep the data entered so far. This is ideal if a complex invoice is being processed and there is not enough time to complete the transaction. The data entered so far can be parked and returned to at a later stage.

There are two main ways to park an invoice. The most common is to decide partway through posting an invoice that you wish to exit and save your work done so far without processing the invoice. To do this, you can use the menu option **Edit > Switch to Document Parking**. This will allow you to save the work you have done so far without the document being posted.

The other option is to start off by using the Invoice Parking function directly, instead of MIRO, using transaction MIR7. This is used in situations where you know that you will not want to process the invoice at this stage. Figure 1.12 shows the initial screen of the MIR7 invoice-parking transaction. Note how similar this is to the MIRO screen.

This is where some implementations misuse the function. Sometimes people interpret the Invoice Parking function as an integral step in the process. It does appear that all invoices could be posted as parked first, and then someone else (perhaps someone more senior) could process the parked invoice into a fully processed invoice. This can be done, and I have seen it used in this way in some implementations, but you have to keep in mind that it was not designed to be used in this way and so is unlikely to function in the way you hoped. In the implementations I have seen, parking was excessive because of overuse of the goods receipt-based invoice verification flag (covered in detail in Section 2.1).

For instance, you can view and monitor parked invoices using transaction MIR6, the Invoice Overview

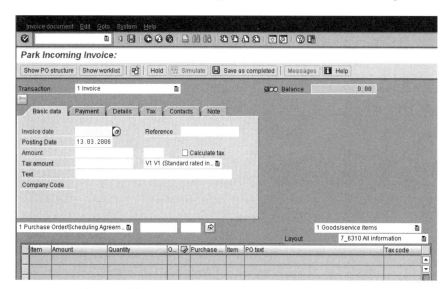

Figure 1.12 Initial Screen of the MIR7 Transaction

function, but there is no ideal transaction that ensures that all parked documents are processed in a timely fashion. This can result in some invoices being overlooked. This is not a failing of the SAP system, but occurs because this is not the purpose of the function. Figure 1.13 shows you how to view or manage parked invoices with transaction MIR6.

Some implementations then tie in workflow functions to manage the processing of parked invoices, and this adds to the complexity.

However, if the whole Invoice Verification function is fully understood, then you are unlikely to find any benefit from using it in this way. The incorrect use of the **GR based Invoice verification flag** often leads to a need to park far more invoices than necessary.

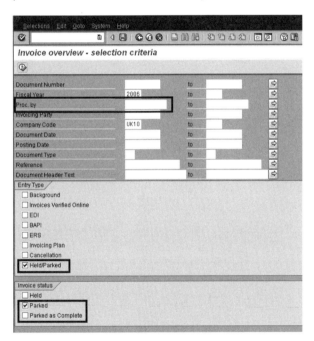

Figure 1.13 MIR6 Transaction Used to Display and Manage Parked Invoices

1.5 Workflow in Invoice Verification

Workflow is a very useful tool within SAP. Some people describe it as event-triggered messaging, but I prefer to refer to it as event-triggered events. Basically, you can use workflow to send a message when an event occurs, or you can trigger an action or another transaction when an event occurs.

The workflow function can be used throughout the SAP functionality and is not restricted to certain events or transactions. However, you will find that in some standard transactions SAP has integrated basic workflow functionality. Invoice verification is one example of this. SAP has a pre-defined workflow template WS20000397, specifically for the management of mismatched invoices.

The standard workflow function in invoice verification is designed to be used to send a workflow message (there is no specific layout for this message; you can word and format it as required) via email or SAPmail to a user The user would be informed that the invoice did not match and be told if it was due to a price or quantity variance. Full details of the purchase order can be included in the message, and further processing can be carried out within the message (to go to the purchase-order change function or the goods-receipt function, directly from within the message).

This function can be very useful when several people are responsible for purchase orders and goods receipts. If staff requirement are low, then it may be easier to just send a photocopy of the invoice in the internal post with the details of the problem.

The workflow process can be configured to use various methods of determining to whom the message should be sent. It could be the user who created the purchase order, the requisitioner, or the person responsible for posting goods receipts at the plant or storage location on the purchase order. If there are complicated rules to be followed, then this can be achieved by basic Advanced Business Application Programming (ABAP) coding. ABAP is SAP's programming language.

All in all, the workflow function is seen as being very useful. It should be considered not only a user-friendly function, but also a good method of ensuring that mismatches are handled quickly and by the appropriate person, without the possibility of omissions due to lost paperwork, or other issues.

As for developing workflow solutions in other areas of invoice verification, or anywhere else in SAP, I have a word of warning. The functionality offered by workflow can dramatically improve many processes, and it can be used to make the system capable of other very useful functions, but it does have an overhead and that is the technical maintenance. This is a small price to pay, but it has to be considered when determining if workflow is appropriate.

It is possible for workflow records to occasionally have technical problems, and this may result in the message not being received or processed by the user. This will leave an unprocessed record that has to be resolved by someone with significant workflow skills. If you multiply this possibility by the number of messages that are transmitted, then this problem-resolution can become almost a full-time task.

Other problems, such as unexpected combinations of data, can also result in unprocessed messages. Thus, the more workflow you use the more need you will have for appropriate support when it goes wrong. This is all man-ageable, but the biggest problem with workflow is that it is so useful that many areas can benefit from its use. This can result in delays during implementations due to the additional design, building, and testing involved.

1.6   Summary

Invoice verification in SAP is a solid and efficient process. But do try wherever possible to use the standard SAP functionality as covered in this chapter. This will ensure that you gain maximum benefits for the least effort.

In Chapter 2, we will be looking at the functionality in more detail, and this should enable you to design an invoice-verification process to suit your needs.

2 Specific Functions in Detail

This chapter will provide the information you need to design and use the main functions within SAP Invoice Verification. Detailed configuration information is described in Chapter 4, and that chapter will also show you how to set up the functionality in a way that best suits your business or your client.

2.1 The Goods Receipt-Based Invoice Verification (GR- Based IV) Flag

This flag indicates that the invoice should be verified against an individual goods receipt rather than a purchase-order line. Using this flag incorrectly can bring about overly complex business processes and can make the SAP Invoice Verification function appear weak. The main design problem is that the flag does not actually do what its name suggests.

Before you consider using this flag, you must realize that it is definitely *not* a flag that you set to ensure that the invoice is verified against goods receipts. Standard invoice-verification in SAP already does this for purchase orders that involve goods receipts. There is no flag to turn this on or off, as it is basic three-way matching, and there would be no point in having an invoice-verification function that does not check the goods receipt data when it is available. Figure 2.1 shows the **GR-based IV** flag on

the item invoice tab of a purchase order (as viewed using transaction ME23N).

What Does the GR-Based IV Flag Do?

To understand the flag's function, you have to think of it as a delivery-note-based invoice-verification flag rather than a goods-receipt-based invoice-verification flag. If you switch it on, then you can verify your invoices against **individual receipts** posted for the purchase-order line instead of a **single line summary of receipts** posted for the purchase-order line. This is very useful if your vendor insists on sending you invoices that detail each delivery instead of a summarized invoice that just shows one line for each line on the purchase order.

There are many reasons, however, why you should try to get the vendor to submit summarized invoices. The main reason is that if you have to match individual receipts, this will take longer. Moreover, some invoices may be blocked for payment, not because we believe that the vendor should not be paid but simply because we cannot match the invoice lines against the receipts we have posted.

Suppose you receive an invoice from a vendor for a total value of €1,000 Euros for a total of 100 pieces of an item. The invoice shows 20 different deliveries for varying quantities, with a delivery-note number alongside

Figure 2.1 GR-based IV Flag on the Item Details of the Purchase Order

each. The total you have received is 100 pieces, and the purchase-order price is €10 each. The total quantity proposed by the system thus matches the total value of the invoice. But, for some reason, the individual delivered quantities do not match (it is possible that your goods-receiving department transposed a couple of delivery note numbers). With the GR-based IV flag set *on*, you have to investigate what happened, and this will take time. So you cannot pay the vendor, even though it is asking for a payment that matches exactly what it is entitled to. In more than one implementation, this has caused vendors to refuse to take any more orders from the company because payments are constantly being made late, or not at all. But if the flag had been set off instead, the invoice could be matched quickly and paid on time.

The Risks of Setting the Flag Off

You should remember that by using three-way matching in invoice verification, the system will not pay a vendor an amount that is not actually owed to that vendor (based on the goods receipts that have occurred and the purchase order price). So, if the flag is set off, there is no greater risk of overpaying the vendor than there is with the flag set on. The only risk that increases is the risk of paying for the *wrong delivery*. Even if this occurs, you will not have overpaid, nor will you pay for the delivery twice (three-way matching will prevent this).

If the total value and quantity match, there is no significant damage. When the other delivery arrives for the same value and quantity, this invoice will be paid and the end result will be the same. If the total value and quantity do not match, the invoice will not balance, and either will be investigated or blocked for payment. Again, no damage is done.

It could be argued that by having the flag set *on* you will highlight errors earlier in the process because there is a more detailed matching during invoice verification. The problem with this argument is that you now will have a more complicated process on every invoice even if it is correct and matches fully, and the vendor will not be overpaid in any case. The low risk, the time saved on every invoice posted, and the likelihood that vendors will be paid on time are advantages to setting the flag off.

The Risks of Setting the Flag On

The main problem here is that you will not be able to post an invoice before you have posted the goods receipt, and you may wish to do so. There can be many benefits from posting an invoice even if the goods receipt has not yet been posted; we cover these benefits later within this chapter.

This is the basic concept behind using the flag: No goods receipt equals no invoice. In this way, you are adding complexity to the process for little or no benefit. If you receive an invoice before the goods receipt has been posted, and you have the flag set on, then you have two main options.

You can exit the transaction and file the paper invoice for re-keying at a later date when the goods receipt has been posted (although, it isn't clear how you will know when this has happened). Alternatively, you can *park* the invoice for later processing. Either way, you now will have to process the invoice at least twice and possibly more often if you think the goods receipt has been posted and it hasn't.

It is important to ensure that the invoice-parking function is not used as a significant step in the invoice-verification process. It has a specific use, and that is to allow the user to exit the transaction before all of the data has been entered or verified, without losing the data entered so far.

This function is designed to be used when you don't have time to finish the transaction (perhaps you have to deal with another call, or you have to go home and you don't want to lose the data you have keyed). It should not be used just because the goods receipt hasn't yet been posted. It is certainly not designed to be used as part of the total process of matching invoices. If you use it this way, you will find that it does not have all the functionality you need, and you will therefore experience various problems.

You may find that some parked invoices are overlooked and remain on file for some time. For example, someone who didn't know that there was already a parked invoice for this item may have posted the invoice again.

Setting the flag on may leave you with less than perfect alternative solutions, whereas if the flag was set off you could post the invoice even though the receipt has not yet been keyed. This has the advantage that you no longer have to process the invoice again once the goods receipt has been keyed. It would have been blocked automatically when it was posted because of the quantity variance caused by the fact that the receipt had not been keyed, and it will remain blocked for payment until the receipt occurs.

There is no automatic release of invoices as such, but if you run the Automatic Release function every night it will release those invoices with blocks that are no longer valid. You run the function using transaction MRBR as a batch job with the **Release automatically** flag set as was seen in Figure 1.11. In this case, if the goods receipt is posted (for the correct quantity) the blocking reason is no longer valid and the invoice will be released for payment (if no other blocks exist).

Thus, with the **GR based IV** flag set "off", an invoice without a goods receipt just needs to be posted once and does not need to be processed manually again when the stock arrives. This situation is much better than having to post the invoice, switch it to parked status, wait for the goods receipt, and then process the invoice again to post it.

In some countries, there is a potential tax benefit from fully posting an invoice even though it does not match correctly (i.e., no receipt has yet been received). This benefit cannot be achieved if the invoice is not posted financially (i.e., by parking the invoice). Please check your local tax laws to verify if this is the case in your country.

On Vs. Off

The advantages of setting the flag off far outweigh the disadvantages. This does not mean that the flag serves no purpose; there are definitely situations where it is necessary. It is essential, for instance, if the vendor insists on matching invoices delivery by delivery. I emphasize insists because I would always try to persuade the vendor not to demand this if at all possible.

There are also certain settings in SAP that will force you to have the GR-based IV flag set on. Self-billing (known as ERS in SAP and covered in Section 2.4) needs this flag to be set on so that the correct data is captured at goods-receipt stage.

Chances are that the business users may prove difficult to convince that they do not need this flag to be set on for the majority of purchase orders.

I have had many a heated debate over this in several implementations, and it has taken many attempts to convince the users to even carry out a test to prove its purpose and use. To avoid this, make sure that you point out very early on in the project that the name of the flag is misleading. Point out that it should be thought of as the *Delivery-note*-based invoice verification and explain the negative effects.

Users will certainly want to carry out goods-receipt-based invoice verification (three-way matching) and so they will be convinced that they need this flag to be set on every time. The problem is that if the flag is used in this way, the complexity involved is wrongly assumed to be due to the complex way that SAP invoice verification works.

If you set up invoice verification correctly and only use this flag when absolutely essential, then SAP Invoice Verification will be seen as an excellent process that is simple to operate and very efficient.

How the Flag Works

If the flag is set on a purchase-order line item and a goods receipt is posted, then a delivery-note number (or bill-of-lading number if appropriate) must be entered at the time of posting (normally using transaction MIGO).

It makes sense to set these fields as mandatory, using the configuration options for MIGO, if you would normally expect all receipts to have some kind of reference-document number. Figure 2.2 shows the MIGO screen and the fields available for this purpose (**Delivery Note** and **Bill of lading**)

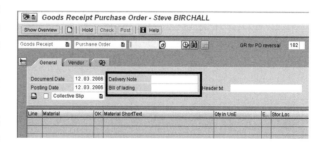

Figure 2.2 Relevant Fields of the MIGO (Goods Receipt) Transaction

The material document now has a unique identification for every goods receipt posted against this purchase order line item. This can be used within invoice verification to display a separate line on the display for every delivery note.

Entering an Invoice for a Purchase Order with the Flag Set On

This results in a slightly different display than normal. You will now see a separate line for each delivery with the delivery-note or bill-of-lading number displayed to enable a full match against the invoice (a bill of lading is a type of shipping document detailing the contents of a consignment).

Figure 2.3 shows the invoice screen for a purchase order with only one line item that has had four separate receipts, each with a different delivery note number. One line is displayed per delivery note instead of the one line per purchase order line because the **GR-based IV** flag is set on the purchase-order line item.

To post the invoice, you must match each delivery contained on the printed invoice from the vendor to a line on the invoice-verification display. You cannot add lines or enter a quantity if the system proposes zero, which indicates that a no goods receipt is awaiting an invoice. This is because you cannot post an invoice for something that has not yet been received when the flag is set on. The quantity you enter against each delivery line displayed on the invoice screen can be less than or equal to the quantity received, but it cannot be more than the quantity received.

If the invoice is for more than the system is proposing, then you either have to park the invoice and then carry out a further receipt before the invoice can be posted or reject the invoice altogether and not post it.

Entering an Invoice for a Purchase Order that Has the Flag Set Off

This results in a normal display with one line per purchase-order line. The quantity proposed on that line will be the quantity remaining to be invoiced. Figure 2.4 shows the invoice screen for a duplicate purchase order that has had the same number of receipts but where the **GR-based IV** flag is set off.

If this is zero or less than the invoice quantity, you simply change it to match the invoice quantity. As long as the invoice lines are mathematically equal to the total invoice value, you can post the invoice.

The system will either leave it available for payment or block it if the tolerances have been exceeded.

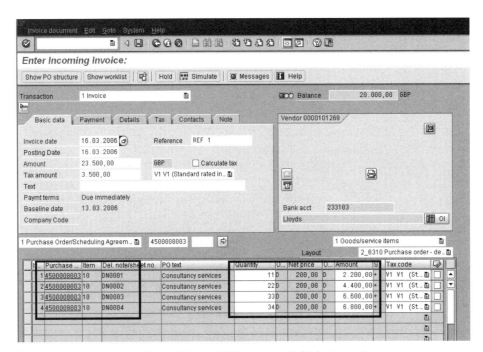

Figure 2.3   Invoice Posting with the GR-Based IV Flag Set On (Multiple Receipts)

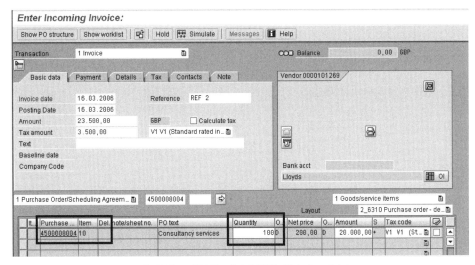

Figure 2.4 Invoice-Posting with GR-Based IV Flag Set Off (Multiple Receipts)

You need not do anything with this invoice after this point. If the extra quantity arrives at a later date, it will be checked again and released if appropriate. This is a much simpler and safer process.

Where is the Flag Set?

The flag is set on the purchase order line (**Delivery** tab) and can be defaulted from the purchasing Info Record if required. Figure 2.5 shows the flag on the Info Record (displayed using transaction ME13).

Figure 2.5 Flag on the Info Record

It can be changed during purchase-order creation or amendment, if required. If a goods receipt has already been posted, then you cannot change the flag. This rarely presents problems, because the invoice can still be posted either way.

2.2 Delivery Charges (Planned and Unplanned)

Delivery charges include freight, customs duty, and insurance. These charges may be known at the time that the purchase order is created, or they may be known at the time of the invoice posting.

It is far better to include these on the purchase order (as pricing conditions) wherever possible. Not only will the costs be posted against the material (as they should), but they will also be processed using the three-way invoice-verification functionality and checked against the vendor's invoice.

Difference Between Planned and Unplanned Delivery Charges

The differences between planned and unplanned are quite clear. Planned delivery charges are added to the material price as pricing conditions on the purchase order, whereas unplanned delivery costs are posted at the invoice-verification stage. Planned charges are visible, controlled, auditable, financially appropriate, and are the correct method of posting such charges.

There are situations, however, where you simply will not know the charges at the time of creating the purchase order. In these cases, you have no choice but to post the charges as unplanned at the invoice-verification stage. It is important to understand the differences between planned and unplanned charges, and especially the financial postings that are involved (i.e. what accounts are used and what values are posted).

A Third Option

Another method often used is to post a separate line on the purchase order for these charges. The main problem with this approach is that there is no connection to the material being purchased unless you reference the material master record. If you do this, you must use an account assignment category to ensure that the costs are posted to a separate account and that the receipt is not seen as a receipt of the material itself. This means that the actual costs are not reflected in the stock account of the material.

You may find this acceptable and decide to handle the posting of these costs later using allocations (these are ways of reallocating costs using financial postings). The standard approach within SAP, however, is to use the planned-charges method where possible and the unplanned option as an alternative.

As with almost anything in SAP, there are many ways of achieving a result. So this third option is one that may be appropriate in your organization. It does have the advantage of providing full three-way matching at invoice time,

and you may want to deliberately separate the costs from the actual material costs.

It can also be added to the purchase order as a new line even after the materials have been received, and so it offers some flexibility. Just make sure that it provides the correct financial updates for your requirements. Figure 2.6 shows an example of a purchase order where the delivery charges are detailed on a separate order line.

Planned Delivery Charges

To use planned delivery charges, you need to ensure that the correct condition types have been configured. The standard condition types are normally more than sufficient, and you will very rarely need to generate new ones. At the most, you would normally just have to ensure that the correct accounts are linked to each condition type via automatic account determination (see Section 3.2).

There is one important setting on the condition type that you need to be aware of: a vendor setting that enables you to specify a different vendor for the delivery charges (as opposed to the main vendor on the purchase order) at goods-receipt stage (MIGO).

If you are not sure you will need to use these options, configure the condition types so that they are switched on and available. That way, you can simply ignore them if you don't need to use them, and the system will use the defaults (i.e., it will assume that the charges will be paid to the same vendor as are the materials charges).

With the option switched on, you can change the freight vendor at purchase-order and goods-receipt

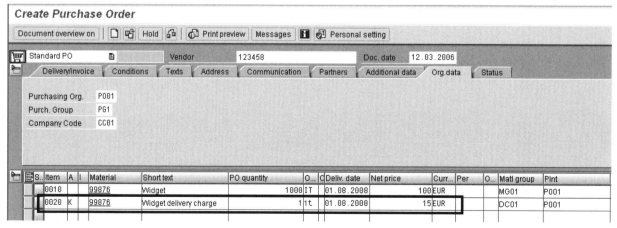

Figure 2.6 Purchase Order Example with Charges Detailed

stages. Figure 2.7 shows the configuration screen of a pricing condition type, with the flag highlighted.

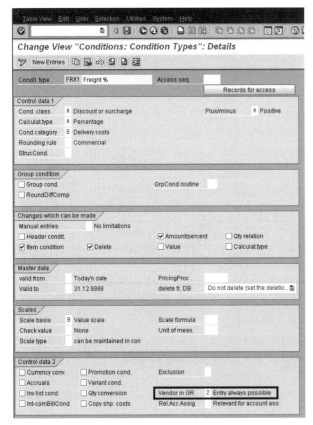

Figure 2.7 Pricing Condition Configuration Screen Showing the Vendor Option

When creating the purchase order, add the appropriate condition types and assign the correct values. If the charge is to be paid to a different vendor, then:

- ▶ Go to the conditions tab of the purchase order
- ▶ Select the condition type by clicking on the select box to the left of the condition type,
- ▶ Click on the details icon (the magnifying glass)

Figure 2.8 shows the condition tab on the purchase order and the icons to select.

You will then see a vendor field, and you can enter the vendor that you will pay the charges to. Figure 2.9 shows the vendor field on the condition type.

If you are not sure which vendor will be used, you can leave this field blank, and it can be entered at goods-receipt stage (if the flag has been set on for this in the configuration of the condition type).

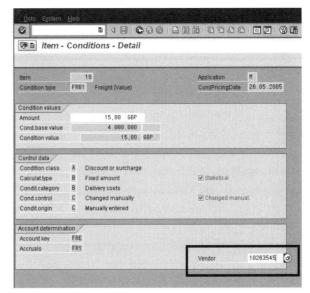

Figure 2.9 Vendor Field on the Condition Type

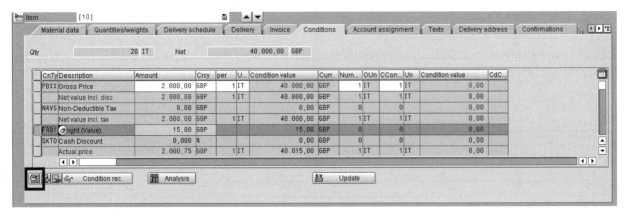

Figure 2.8 Conditions Tab on the Purchase Order

You have two main options when dealing with additional charges like this. You can either enter the delivery condition types on the item line conditions of the purchase order, or you can enter them as header conditions by clicking on the conditions tab of the header. Figure 2.10 shows the **Header Conditions** tab on the purchase order.

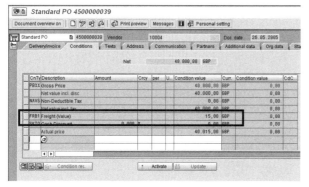

Figure 2.10 Header Conditions Tab on the Purchase Order Header

The main difference is in how the costs are then apportioned. Header delivery costs are spread evenly across the items on the purchased order, while item delivery costs are only applied to that item. If the charges relate to an item, then post them as item conditions, and if the charge is per purchase order, then post them as header conditions.

If the delivery condition types don't appear on the header or item-conditions tab, then you need your MM consultant who deals with purchasing configuration to ensure that the condition types are included in the correct price calculation schema.

There are several delivery-condition types, and you should choose the appropriate condition type for the purpose. Some involve a single charge that does not vary according to the quantity or value, and some are proportional.

These condition types can have pricing scales: One charge for up to x items, and a different charge for over x items and so on. They also can be set up so that they relate to volume or weight if appropriate. These condition types should be added to the purchase order before the goods receipt. They cannot be added afterwards.

When the goods receipt is posted (normally using transaction MIGO), the system will assume that the delivery charges are now to be available for invoicing. If the condition type has been configured correctly, you will also see an additional tab in MIGO that will allow you to enter or change the vendor responsible for the charges.

Posting Planned Delivery Charges in Invoice Verification

In invoice verification, you have to clearly indicate whether the invoice you are posting includes delivery costs. Your choices are as follows:

► The invoice has the material charges and delivery charges combined
► The invoice has material charges only
► The invoice has delivery charges only

The options are selected from a pull-down list on the main screen of transaction MRO. Figure 2.11 shows the pull-down list.

If the invoice has only one vendor (i.e., if both delivery charges and material charges are to be paid to the same vendor) then you can leave the vendor-number field to default from the purchase order. Just use the drop-down list to select the appropriate option.

However, if you are posting the delivery charges only, and if they are being paid to a vendor other than the one responsible for the items being purchased, you must enter in the vendor field on the MIRO transaction the vendor being paid for the delivery charges.

Enter the purchase-order number, and the screen will then show the values that the system has calculated are due, using the selection you made to indicate whether delivery charges or material charges are to be included.

The advantage of this approach is that it introduces genuine three-way matching. The delivery charges will only be shown if they have been received, and the value will be the value entered on the purchase order. As with a normal invoice, you can (and should) change the details proposed by the system to match those on the paper invoice. The system will then carry out the normal checks to see if the invoice balances and to determine if payment should be blocked.

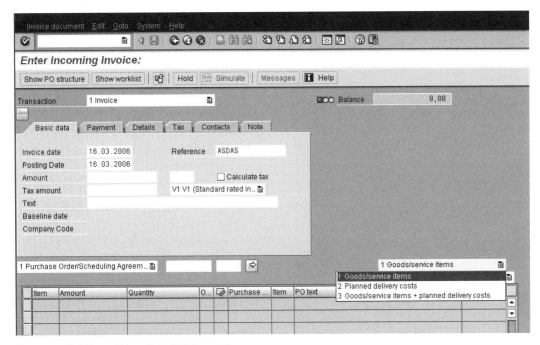

Figure 2.11 Pull-Down List on the MIRO Transaction

The delivery charges are posted to the stock account at the goods-receipt stage (subject to the rules regarding standard or moving average price controls, as discussed in Section 3.5). Any variances arising from a difference in invoice value will cause correction postings to the stock account (again subject to the standard or moving average price controls).

The appropriate goods receipt/invoice receipt (GR/IR) clearing accounts will be updated, separate clearing accounts for the delivery charges and material charges will be used. See Section 4.3 to learn how to configure these.

I recommend that you use planned delivery charges wherever possible. If you are unable to enter the delivery charges or vendor until invoice verification, then unplanned delivery charges should be used.

Unplanned Delivery Charges

If no delivery charges have been stored on the purchase order and delivery charges are contained on the invoice (this may be an agreed process with the vendor) then you have to enter them manually at the invoice-verification stage. If you need to enter delivery charges that are not included on the purchase order during invoice verification, then you have two main options:

You can add an additional line and assign the charge to a specific general-ledger account. You can enter the value in the unplanned delivery charges field, as shown in Figure 2.12.

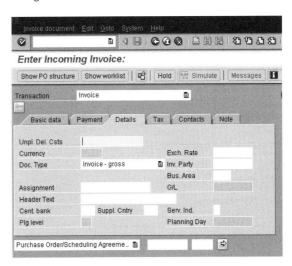

Figure 2.12 Unplanned Delivery Costs Field on the »Details« Tab

The advantage of the second of these two methods is that associated functionality was designed for this purpose. On the other hand, merely adding an extra line to the invoice is perfectly acceptable if you believe that the financial postings will meet requirements.

By using the field provided instead of a separate line, you have the advantage of choosing to spread the charges equally across the invoice lines (by value). You need to realize, though, that the cost is not spread only across the lines on this current invoice; it will be spread across the total invoiced value to date for this purchase order.

There is an option that is controlled by configuration (see Section 4.4), and this indicates how you want to handle the unplanned delivery charges entered in this field. You can either spread them across the invoice lines, or you can have them posted to separate accounts automatically. This setting is controlled at the company-code level, so you should decide to use one method for all invoices relating to that company code.

One disadvantage of unplanned delivery charges is that they cannot be checked using three-way matching. As a result, values entered here will be passed for payment as long as the rest of the invoice is fully matched within tolerances.

A Third Option

There is another option available if you must control invoices for additional charges by three-way matching. You can use a subsequent debit instead of using the unplanned delivery charges field.

To do this, you raise the subsequent debit (as detailed in Section 2.8) and enter the charge manually against the relevant item lines, splitting the costs in whatever proportion you want to. You can even post these against a different vendor if required, by changing the defaulted vendor in the details tab of the invoice-header screen.

Remember that subsequent debits are classed as *value-only* invoices, so this additional invoice will not affect the quantity invoiced but only the value invoiced.

This method has the advantage of passing the costs directly to the material stock accounts. Moreover, the invoice will be blocked if this additional value exceeds the purchase order's value. I prefer this option to the use of the unplanned-delivery-costs field, and I would suggest that you try this on your test system. You may find it the best way to handle your unplanned delivery charges.

2.3   Tolerances

Many tolerances that relate to invoice verification are available, and you don't have to configure them all. Some of them may not be relevant for your implementation. It is important to understand is that you have to think of these tolerances as controlling if an invoice should be blocked. They are generally not used to determine if an invoice can be posted (saved).

Why Have Tolerances?

What is the point of tolerances? While it is true that you would not want vendors to be overpaid for any reason, you should consider the true cost of investigating small differences.

Let's use an example. A vendor has invoiced you for a total of €10,000 for a purchase order by which you received 100 items at a price of €99.90 for each item. This has resulted in a difference of €10. If you calculate the true cost of passing this invoice to the buyer for investigation, and the buyer contacting the vendor, then changing the purchase order to reflect the correct price, and the invoice-verification clerk then re-matching the invoice, it certainly comes to far more than €10.

It is for your company to decide if this true cost is worth the effort, and this decision may well be influenced by the general standard of vendors that you use. It may be acceptable that your vendors take advantage of this tolerance, or it may be that the sheer frequency of such small differences makes it unacceptable.

That is exactly what the tolerances are there for: so the implementation team can work with the financial department to decide what, if any, differences will be allowed.

What Kind of Tolerances are There?

It is also important to realize that the tolerances in invoice verification relate to more than prices or values. There are tolerances that relate to dates, and one such tolerance is linked to the delivery date. This is very useful when a vendor has sent an invoice in too early, something often done deliberately.

The *delivery-date tolerance* can be used to check the invoice date against the requested delivery date. A vendor will sometimes send the goods and invoice early, and without this tolerance the invoice would normally be paid because the invoice quantity would match the goods- received quantity. This special tolerance however, would check the invoice date and delivery date and block the invoice for payment because of the early invoice.

Early invoices cost your company in two of the following ways:

▶ You lose cash-flow due to early payment.
▶ You have to pay to store the goods until the date you actually need them.

Special Tolerances

Certain special tolerances don't seem important at first but in fact are extremely useful. One example is the **Moving Average variance** tolerance. If you do not use moving average prices (MAP) in your implementation, then this tolerance is not required. Section 3.5 gives more information on moving average prices.

As covered earlier, when an invoice is posted with a variance in value, the financial postings still occur but the invoice is blocked for payment. This can cause major problems if you are using MAP, because the incorrect invoice price will affect the MAP even though the invoice did not match and was blocked.

For instance, if you have a material that has a MAP of €100 each, and you post an invoice with a value of €1,000 each for this material (perhaps because of a genuine keying error by the vendor or invoice-verification clerk), the MAP will be increased significantly even though the invoice will be blocked for payment.

That is why SAP has provided this tolerance. You can set it (normally with a reasonably large tolerance) so that when an invoice is posted for an item, a warning message is displayed indicating that posting this invoice will cause a significant change in the MAP.

This can prevent future problems if the item is consumed at the potentially artificial cost. Remember that if the invoice is subsequently corrected, this will not correct the values used in any postings that occurred between the initial invoice posting and any correction.

> **Note:** The same tolerance is used during goods-receiving to indicate significant changes to the MAP caused by a goods receipt at a value different from the current MAP, due to a different purchase order price.

Other Tolerances

Another useful tolerance is related to those invoices that contain lines that do not relate directly to a purchase order. These cannot be three-way matched, and so SAP provides a tolerance that can be set to block an invoice line that does not relate to a purchase order if it exceeds a certain value. Another user to ensure that the invoice is valid can then check this blocked invoice line.

One special tolerance that must be used correctly is the one called "Form small differences automatically." It is vital that this is used only to allow extremely small differences, such as rounding errors; otherwise it will allow invoices to be paid even though they do not match.

It is quite normal for this tolerance to be set to a value as small as €1, which is a typical variance caused by tax postings such as VAT. This tolerance is also unique because it does not affect whether the invoice is blocked.

It influences the mathematical check carried out to ensure that all invoice lines and taxes add up to the total invoice value that has been entered. I have seen this tolerance set to very high values by mistake, and this has always resulted in many problems throughout the invoice process.

Configuring the Tolerances

Configuring the tolerances is covered in Section 4.4 in detail, but there are some tips that can help get you started.

First, you must ensure that you have all of the required tolerances set up for your company code or codes. I find that the easiest way to do this is to copy the standard tolerances that SAP has configured for the company code 0001. This way, you will at least have the full set, and all that you will have to do is to change the values of the tolerances to suit your requirements. Some transactions will expect certain tolerance keys to exist for the company code being used and will report errors if they do not exist.

For the development/play client, I normally copy the following tolerance keys from company code 0001, shown in Figure 2.13. This will at least allow you to use the system before you configure the final tolerance settings.

Co...	Company Name	TlKy	Description
0001	SAP A.G.	AN	Amount for item without order reference
0001	SAP A.G.	AP	Amount for item with order reference
0001	SAP A.G.	BD	Form small differences automatically
0001	SAP A.G.	BR	Percentage OPUn variance (IR before GR)
0001	SAP A.G.	BW	Percentage OPUn variance (GR before IR)
0001	SAP A.G.	DQ	Exceed amount: quantity variance
0001	SAP A.G.	DW	Quantity variance when GR qty = zero
0001	SAP A.G.	KW	Var. from condition value
0001	SAP A.G.	PP	Price variance
0001	SAP A.G.	PS	Price variance: estimated price
0001	SAP A.G.	ST	Date variance (value x days)
0001	SAP A.G.	VP	Moving average price variance

Figure 2.13 Basic Set of Tolerances Used as a Starting Point

Each tolerance key is described in Section 4.4.

Error Messages Resulting from Tolerances

To ensure that you have the correct error-message settings for each tolerance, you can set the message to an "E" or a "W." Messages set to "E" are treated as errors and will not allow the process to continue. Messages set to "W" are treated as warnings and can be ignored to allow the process to continue.

You can also configure different error message settings for each user or group of users, so that one user gets an "E" message and another gets a "W" message.

Figures showing the settings and full details are contained in Section 4.2. As an example of how this can be used, you may wish to prevent certain tolerances from being allowed unless they have been authorized. To achieve this, you need to set the error message to an "E" for "normal" users but set the message to a "W" for a supervisor.

When users get the "E" message preventing the invoice from being processed, they must ask a supervisor to post the invoice. The supervisor will just get a warning message, but will be allowed to continue.

2.4   ERS (Evaluated Receipt Settlement)

ERS amounts to self-billing. Self-billing occurs when the vendor will not submit an invoice and we will send the payment to the vendor based on what we have ordered and received. This is a very useful function that will save a lot of time and effort if used appropriately. It is designed to be used with vendors with whom you have good business relationships, and it works even better when used

for inter- or intra-company purchases between different elements of your own business. The concept is very simple and follows standard business processes, even though it appears to be quite different from the normal invoice verification.

How Does ERS Work?

If you use the standard three-way matching within invoice verification, the system compares the invoice value against the quantity received so far, multiplied by the price on the purchase order. If the vendor's invoice matches this, then it is passed for payment.

For the system to match the invoice, it must know the values and quantities that already are due to the vendor. If the system knows these details, then why wait for the vendor's invoice? Why not just send a payment at the agreed-upon time (according to the payment terms) for the values it has calculated? The benefit of this approach is that you would not need to use an invoice verification department at all, and there would (in theory) be no blocked invoices.

How Safe is the Process?

This process might appear to be slightly risky. What if you overpaid the vendor? They would not be in a hurry to send the money back.

Then again, this functionality is really designed for those vendors that you know and trust (within reason). After all, you have full control over the purchase-order price, and you actually carry out the goods receipt and indicate exactly what you have received.

The possibility of overpaying is therefore low, and the benefits are high. Fewer people are required in the process, you pay on time, and you are therefore more able to negotiate better prices (in fact some vendors will offer better deals just because you are prepared to use self-billing).

ERS for Inter- or Intra-Company Scenarios

If you are using purchase orders to buy and sell between different parts of your own organization, then ERS should be considered for the settlement of any related invoices. It seems strange when I see organizations buying from parts of their own business, generating invoices and matching them, and having such problems as blocked invoices. If you really must invoice in this way, then do consider ERS as it will eliminate wasted time and energy.

The ERS Process

The process is not complicated. You flag the vendor as being relevant for ERS. Figure 2.14 shows the flag on the purchasing-data view of the vendor master record.

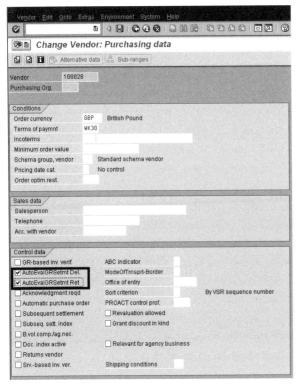

Figure 2.14 Evaluated-Receipt Flag on Vendor Master Record

This flag is then passed (via the Info Record if used) to the purchase-order lines. But the flag on the Info Record is only set if you want this combination of material and vendor not to have ERS. If the flag is set on in the Vendor Master, then all purchases will be treated as ERS relevant unless you set the **No ERS** flag on the Info Record. Figure 2.15 shows the **No ERS** flag on the purchasing data of the Info Record.

When using this flag, the system will insist on a valid VAT code being specified in the purchase order (if VAT is relevant in the country involved).

The system needs this because there will be no opportunity to enter this later, as the invoice-verification function is not relevant. At the goods-receipt stage, the system creates an additional record (it is not a normal document

record, but one that is only needed by the settlement program). This record is used to speed up the process when the settlement program is used. Instead of searching through all goods receipts for relevant records, it can just search through these specially designed records.

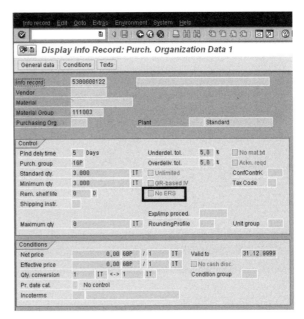

Figure 2.15 No ERS Flag on the Info Record

The ERS Settlement Transaction

The ERS settlement transaction (MRRL) is run periodically (normally monthly). This actually mimics the invoice-verification transaction. It creates an invoice document as MIRO does, but it uses the known quantities and values to complete the details of this document that would be manually entered in the MIRO transaction. The invoice will not be blocked for quantity or price reasons, because these are derived from the purchase order and goods receipt and so will match exactly.

Other blocking factors could be applied, such as stochastic blocks (described in Section 4.7). Figure 2.16 shows the selection screen of MRRL.

The settlement program has an output type attached to it that will produce a printed (or faxed, emailed, etc.) document that details the transactions being settled.

This output goes to the vendor so that it will know what the payment covers. The settlement does not directly trigger a payment. It merely creates the usual invoice-verification record. This record will be considered in the next appropriate payment run, taking into account the associated payment terms to ensure that it is not paid too early (or too late). The posting date of goods-receipt range should be entered, and these dates should be exact to ensure that there is no overlap or gap in the dates of each run.

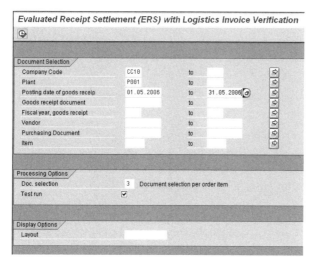

Figure 2.16 Selection Screen of the ERS Settlement Transaction (MRRL)

2.5   Invoice Reduction

This functionality may be useful in certain implementations, but I don't see it as a generally used function. It fulfills a specific task and is only relevant when a mismatch occurs. It is only used when you class the vendor's invoice as being incorrect when a mismatch occurs and where you want the difference to be balanced out with a credit note automatically. This means that the scenarios where this is appropriate are rare.

What Does Invoice Reduction Do?
It is easier to describe invoice reduction by using the following example.

A vendor has sent in an invoice for more than you were expecting and for a higher value than the value of the goods received against the relevant purchase order. You have contacted the vendor, and they have agreed that the invoice is wrong. In normal circumstances, you would have two options: Ask the vendor to send in a corrected invoice, or post the invoice and await a credit note.

With invoice reduction you have a third option: you can post the invoice and the credit note at the same time, in one transaction. The result is an invoice that matches, because the overcharge is balanced out by the credit note.

The invoice can be cleared, and the payment would be for the difference between the invoice value and the credit-note value. This can save a lot of time and effort, but you would need the consent of the vendor to use this function. You will have to verify with your financial department whether posting an invoice in this manner is acceptable.

If you want to post the incorrect invoice without using invoice reduction, then the process would involve the posting of the incorrect invoice with the potential to corrupt the MAP if it is used. The invoice would be blocked for payment, and you would have to wait for a credit note to be received from the vendor.

Then you would have to post the credit note onto the system and finally run the MRBR transaction to clear the invoice for payment. The other option—not posting the invoice at all until the correct one has arrived from the vendor—means that you will have to cancel the invoice verification for this invoice and wait until the new one arrives, leaving open the possibility that a further mismatch might occur.

Many organizations opt to simply await a replacement invoice because this does not present any significant problems. It is strange, though, that out of all of the SAP implementations that I have been involved in, not one of them has used the invoice-reduction process.

The Invoice-Reduction Process
For this process, you post the invoice in the normal way using MIRO. When the difference is identified, you need to decide if you want to post it and block the payment or—if you are sure that it is a vendor error—post it using invoice reduction. If you wish to treat it as a vendor error, then choose the layout **Invoice Reduction** from the list of layout options on the **Enter Incoming Invoice** screen, as shown in Figure 2.17.

You will then be able to enter a **correction ID** in the appropriate field (you will need to scroll to the right to see this field). The list will contain options that have been configured, and there would normally be one that indicates **vendor error**.

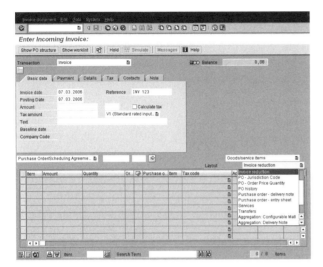

Figure 2.17 Invoice-Reduction Selection from the Pull-Down List

It is important that you not enter the corrected data from the vendor's invoice into the **Amount** and **Qty** fields as you would normally do. Just leave these as they are defaulted by the system. You must now enter the amount and quantity from the vendor's invoice in the specially provided fields for invoice reduction.

These fields are labeled **Invoice amount acc. to vendor**, and **Invoice qty acc. to vendor**. This is why you need to specify the invoice-reduction layout; otherwise these fields would not be displayed. Figure 2.18 shows the special fields on the invoice-reduction layout.

Entering the data in these additional fields enables the system to calculate the variance value to use in the automatic credit that it will create. When you press **Enter**, you will see a window indicating the amount that will be reduced by the posting. As long as the value entered in these special fields (minus tax as usual) corresponds to the invoice value entered in the **Basic data** tab (taking tax into consideration), then the balance should be zero, and the invoice should post successfully.

The Financial Posting of the Difference

The difference will be posted to a special clearing account that is determined by automatic account determination using the transaction event key RKA. See Section 3.2 for details.

Ensure that the finance department has specified which general-ledger account should be used, and request the account to be set up to accept automatic postings. The credit note that is automatically created also posts to the same clearing account, thereby balancing the posting.

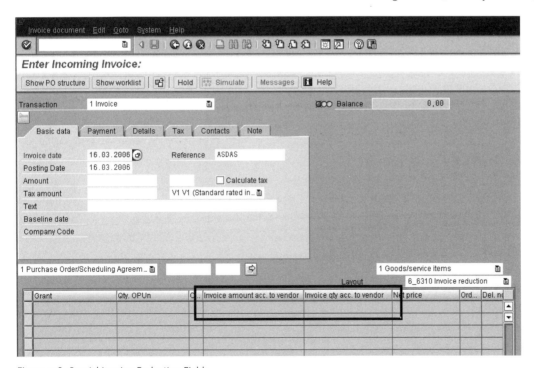

Figure 2.18 Special Invoice-Reduction Fields

> **Note:** Any credit posted via this function is not reflected in the stock account. The transaction is seen as a value correction relating to the payment of the vendor and not a variance of the cost of the materials received. So there is no impact on the MAP or price-variance account for the material.

The system sees the variance as an invoicing error, and the end result is that the postings at goods-receipt stage were correct and so do not need to be adjusted. The payment to the vendor will also be for the price of the materials multiplied by the quantity received, and so again no correction is necessary.

2.6   Pipeline and Consignment Stock Settlement

Invoice payments for pipeline materials and consignment stocks are treated in the same way. The basic concept that applies to both is that you only pay for the consumption of these items, and there is no purchase order to match against an invoice. Consignment purchase orders exist but are not valuated, and no invoices are matched against them; they are merely used to request a replenishment of the stock.

In effect, the vendors are paid via a form of ERS. The basic process is that the details of the consumption are collected from goods-movement records, and the value of the items (stored on special Info Records) is multiplied by the quantity involved in the movement. This gives the amount due to the vendor. The settlement program is run periodically and creates an invoice-verification record available for payment for the value concerned, as it does in ERS.

I have seen implementations where modifications have been made to allow invoices to be posted against consignment purchase orders, but this is not recommended, and many problems surface later on due to the non-standard functionality.

The consignment purchase orders are meant to be unvalued and are only designed to be records that control the replenishment of stock. After all, the basic con-

cept is that you pay for the items as you use them, and this practice is not normally linked to the quantity you ordered from the vendor.

If you want to link the purchase order to the invoice, then you must ask yourself if consignment stock is appropriate. Normal purchase orders may be more appropriate in this case.

Consignment Stock

Consignment stock is stock that you have available to use as and when you wish to. The stock remains the property of the vendor until it is used and does not appear in your accounts in any way. You pay the vendor for any stock that you have used since the last settlement. Purchase orders are used, but only to request the vendor to replenish the stock.

The goods receipts against these purchase orders do not cause any financial postings because the stock is still owned by the vendor. Financial postings only occur when the stock is consumed, written-off, scrapped, or transferred to your own stock.

These movements cause the value to be posted to the appropriate liability account awaiting settlement, which transfers the value from the liability account to the vendor account as an open item when the settlement occurs.

Something that appears strange at first is that any stock-count losses cause financial postings, and yet the stock does not belong to us. If we have lost some of the vendor's stock, we are liable to pay for it, and so we effectively have to treat it as being consumed. Therefore we owe the vendor for the stock we lost.

The consignment settlement transaction (MRKO) operates in a manner similar to the ERS transaction, and it is equally important to specify exact date ranges that do not overlap or have gaps.

You can use it either to display or settle the liabilities by using the appropriate flags. You must also indicate if you wish to settle consignment stock liabilities, pipeline liabilities or both by using the appropriate flags. Figure 2.19 shows the selection screen used for consignment stock settlement (and also for pipeline settlement) and the flags to indicate which is to be settled.

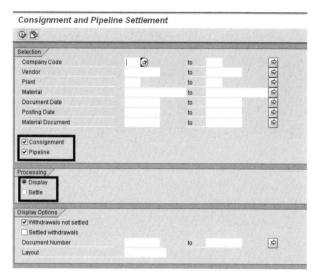

Figure 2.19 Consignment Settlement Transaction

Pipeline Stock

Pipeline materials are used for items you consume or sell, that you do not obtain via a purchase order, and where stock availability is assumed to be unlimited.

This category has been designed for utilities such as gas, electricity, or water, but is equally suited to anything that is available in unlimited quantity, that does not involve a purchase order, and that you pay for as you use it. One of the biggest advantages is that this allows you to include these items on bills of materials (BOMs) and therefore collect consumption figures and post these costs to the material, if required.

Pipeline stock can be used for other situations. You are not limited to materials that are true pipeline materials. It could, for instance be used use to manage royalty and license payments. They do act in a very similar manner to pipeline materials, because these license fees and royalty payments are available in unlimited quantities.

We don't hold them in stock, we don't have to order them from the vendor, and they only have to be paid for as you use them. You can therefore include them in BOMs, etc., and capture the costs and consumption automatically, if required.

Pipeline liabilities are settled in the same way that consignment materials are (in fact by the same program), and the only real difference between these and consignment materials is that they do not have stock levels or purchase orders. The value is stored on pipeline Info Records, and these are used to calculate the liability to the vendor for

each item consumed. The transaction MRKO is used, the same transaction that it used for consignment stock settlement.

2.7 Invoicing Plans

This functionality has been designed to be used for payments that are not directly linked to standard goods receipts or service confirmation. They enable you to use purchase orders for some situations where you may have been tempted to use a financial posting instead.

This allows you to view such expenditures in the purchasing totals and reports. It is most likely to be used by the purchasing department for special purchases such as leases, rentals, or anything that has staged payments. There are two main types of invoicing plans:

▸ Suitable for regular payments (periodic invoicing plans)

▸ Suitable for partial payments of varying percentage spread over time (partial invoicing plans).

Although they are both invoicing plans, they are treated differently, and it is best to deal with each separately.

In both cases, it is possible to post invoices as the payments are to be made, without involving purchase orders. Even though this works from an invoice point of view, it does miss out on valuable information.

For instance, with no purchase order, the values involved would not show up in any reports on spend that obtain their information from purchase orders. Purchase orders also indicate future spending and commitments, and so this information would not be available.

We would not be able to see that we have committed to spend x amount every month for N months with vendor Y for item Z. With a purchase order, we can do all of this while using the other related processes, such as, authorization of the order and visibility of cash-flow.

Periodic Invoicing Plans

Periodic invoicing plans are designed for set value payments paid regularly, such as monthly, weekly, or annually. They are ideal for payments such as rentals, leases, or insurance.

Many organizations use the regular payments options available in the financial module of SAP, but this does not contain all of the information. Therefore, a purchase order is involved. Instead of just having one value for each item, we have a value for each payment for each item and details of when each payment should be made.

This would then allow a matching against regular invoices (if sent by the vendor). Better still, it can be used to trigger regular payments without waiting for an invoice using transaction MRIS (many vendors would not invoice for regular payments in any case).

Figure 2.20 shows the selection screen of the MRIS transaction. Note the **Test run** flag, which allows you to see the actions without updating anything.

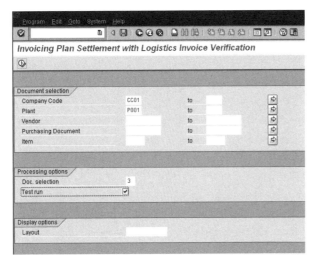

Figure 2.20 Selection Screen of the Invoicing Plan Settlement Transaction (MRIS)

Partial Invoicing Plans

Partial invoicing plans are designed to be used when the payments to be made to the vendor are not regular amounts and when they are paid at irregular times, perhaps depending on specific events or stages. The most appropriate example of this would be a situation where a vendor will be paid according to progress.

A building contract may have "staged payments" such as a percentage at commencement of the work, a further percentage when stage one is reached, further payments at each of the following stages, and perhaps a final payment several months after completion.

Payments such as these are normally only managed within the finance department because they are irregular and infrequent, and it would be too difficult to issue separate purchase orders for each payment. Using a partial payment plan could make the use of a purchase order feasible and add the associated benefits of visibility of the commitment and spending.

How Does the Process Work?

The purchase order is issued as normal, but you must select a non-valuated receipt or de-select the goods-receipt flag altogether on the **Delivery** tab of the purchase order item. Figure 2.21 shows the flags on the **Delivery** tab.

Invoicing plans cannot be used where a valuated receipt occurs. When you have entered the purchase order details, you click on the **Invoice** tab on the item details section and then select **Invoicing plan**.

Figure 2.22 shows the **Invoicing plan** icon, which offers the option of choosing the appropriate invoicing-plan type.

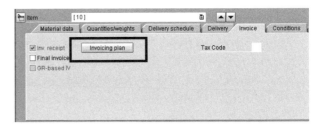

Figure 2.22 Invoicing plan Icon on the Invoice Tab of the Purchase Order

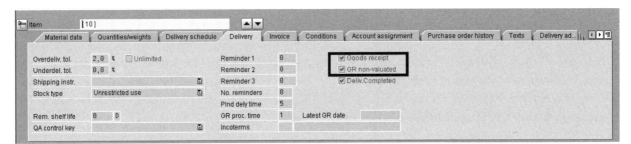

Figure 2.21 Receipt flags on the Delivery Tab of the Purchase Order

The number and type of options presented will depend on what has been configured, but you would expect to see at least two options: partial and periodic.

When you have selected the appropriate type, you will be presented with a new window in which you can enter the details of the invoice plan. Some dates can be defaulted automatically if you have configured this option correctly. Figure 2.23 shows the new window that allows you to enter full details of the invoicing dates.

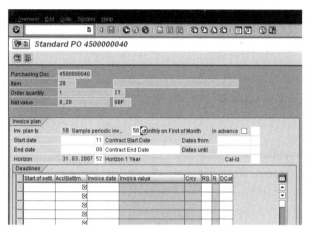

Figure 2.23 Invoice Plan Details Screen

A partial invoicing plan will allow you to enter dates and percentages that relate to the various stages of payments. You can leave the data blank window if the details are not yet known, and you should enter the stage details as and when they are known.

You can either enter a percentage of the value for each stage, or the actual value. The total percentage must add up to 100% and must equal the value of the item line.

A periodic invoicing plan will allow you to enter the payment schedule using regular or irregular dates. It is important to remember that the net price you entered against the item line is actually the individual payment amount, not the total. So if the payment is €100 every month for 10 months, the "net price" on the item line must be €100, not €1,000.

Invoice Verification Relating to Invoicing Plans
You can simply post invoices against the purchase order in the same way as any other purchase order. It is often better, though, to use a self-billing approach, particularly for periodic invoice plans.

If you use MIRO to post the invoice, then the system will match the invoice against any goods receipts that have been posted (if the GR flag was set on the PO line), or matched against the dates of the stages or periods if no GR flag was set.

If you want to use self-billing, you can use the MRIS transaction (Invoicing Plan Settlement with Logistics Invoice Verification). Simply enter the selection criteria and execute the transaction (ideally in test mode initially). See Figure 2.21 for the selection screen of MRIS.

Basic Configuration for Invoicing Plans
You need to ensure that your materials-management team has configured the different types of invoicing plans that you need to be available for use. They will also need to configure any automatic date calculations such as start dates and periods.

There is no specific configuration in logistics invoice verification. The invoices are managed the same as normal purchase order related invoices.

2.8 Subsequent Debits and Credits

The biggest problem with this functionality is the terminology used. *Subsequent* does not explain exactly what is involved. If you substitute the words *value only* for subsequent, it helps clarify it. You are, in fact, posting a value only credit or debit.

Subsequent debits and credits are used to correct or amend invoiced values without affecting the quantities involved.

Suppose, vendor A sends in an invoice for 10 items at €15 each and later realizes that the price was wrong and you should have been charged €14 each. You cannot post a normal credit note, because this would involve a return of the items involved and in this case the quantity is to remain unaffected.

You therefore have to post a credit note that will only affect the value, i.e., a subsequent (or value-only) credit. A subsequent debit is the same process, but in this case the vendor is charging an increased value for the items.

Posting a Subsequent Credit
The normal invoice-verification transaction (MIRO) is used to post a subsequent credit.

Select **subsequent credit** from the pull-down list in the transaction field. This will ensure that the quantity involved in the credit posting will remain unaffected. Figure 2.24 shows the pull-down list that allows you to specify a subsequent credit posting instead of an invoice.

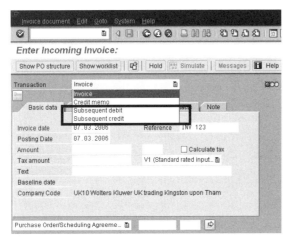

Figure 2.24 Pull-Down List of MIRO Showing Subsequent Credit and Debit Options

Then follow these steps:

1. Enter the invoice details as normal, entering the total value of the credit (including taxes), and specify the tax value (or select the **Calculate tax** flag).
2. Enter the total value of the credit that applies to each line (not the value per item). For instance, if there is a one line invoice and the credit value is €100, enter 100 in the **Amount** field on the invoice line. If the total credit was €100, and this was to be spread equally over two lines, enter €50 on each invoice line.
3. Enter a quantity, even though no items are being returned and this is a "value-only" credit. This quantity will be used to calculate how the value will be spread. A subsequent credit of €100 for 100 items results in a price difference of €1 an item.

The quantity is also important where the credit relates to a specific quantity other than the actual quantity invoiced so far.

For example, the vendor has agreed that two of the items sent were substandard and has agreed to give you a credit of €200 to compensate you. The order and invoice was for 100 items, and so you would enter the value of 200 and the quantity of two (replacing the quantity of 100 that would be defaulted by the system). This way, the postings will reflect that two of the items now cost €100 less (each).

This price variance will be posted to the stock account (if the material uses MAP and if there are, in this case, at least two items still in stock) or to a price-variance account (these postings are explained in more detail in Section 3.5).

The total quantity invoiced remains unaffected (because this is a value-only credit) but the purchase order history will be updated to reflect the subsequent credit and the values will be reflected in detail.

Posting a Subsequent Debit

To post a subsequent debit, follow the same process as when posting a subsequent credit, except this time you are posting a value-only invoice. Figure 2.24 shows the pull-down list where this option can be selected. This function is used where a vendor indicated that the price on an invoice was too low and the vendor had to send you an additional (or subsequent) debit.

It can also be used to post additional charges such as delivery charges, especially if you do not wish to use planned or unplanned delivery charges (as detailed in Section 2.3).

The basic concept is that you are being invoiced for additional values, but the total quantity that has been invoiced remains unaffected.

As with subsequent credits, you still have to specify the quantity that is affected by the debit so that the exact affect of the debit can be correctly reflected against the items.

The purchase-order history will reflect the extra debit in full detail.

Posting a Normal Credit

This kind of credit will affect the quantity invoiced as well as the value. It should only be used if the relevant items are either returned to the vendor or are to be treated as if you have never received them.

The process is the same as posting an invoice, only this time the values are reversed. That is essentially the only difference between a credit note and an invoice. The process, the checks, and even the screens are the same, but the signs are reversed (negative to positive and vice versa). Select the credit-memo option from the pull down list in MIRO, then do the following:

1. Enter the details as you would for an invoice.
2. When you have entered the details and specified the purchase-order number, the system will suggest the quantity and value of the items that have already been invoiced.
3. Then change these to reflect the quantities and values that you are receiving credit for, or even enter them if the fields are blank.

The end result is a posting of the credit to the vendor's account, the credit record as an audit trail, and an entry on the purchase-order history to show the details of the credit.

2.9 Purchase-Order Texts

This is a little-used function that can be very useful indeed. It is not as complicated to set up and configure, as it appears. It essentially enables texts from the purchase-order header to be displayed during invoice verification. Ways to configure certain texts to be displayed are covered in Chapter 4.

The Basic Process

The person creating a purchase order can enter texts in many places on the order, and each of the different kinds of texts can be used for different purposes. For example, the **Item** text on the purchase order can be printed along with the full order details when the document is printed, faxed, emailed, etc. to the vendor. This text can give the vendor more information relating to the item being ordered. There are other texts at item level, and these can be used to store and display internal notes and memos that are not seen by the vendor but can be viewed by internal staff.

There are also header texts, which are used in the same way as item texts but with the information relating to the whole purchase order and not individual items. The person creating a purchase order can store at the header level text that can be printed on the order or can be used as an internal memo. Texts such as these are often underutilized, but they can be very helpful in invoice verification. Figure 2.25 shows the header texts on a typical purchase order.

If configured correctly, selected texts can be displayed at the invoice verification stage. When the purchase-order reference has been keyed into the MIRO transaction, the system checks to see if there are any texts on that purchase order that are flagged as relevant to invoice verification. If there are any, the system will use a pop-up window to inform the user that relevant texts exist. The user can then ask to view the texts from within that window. The text will be displayed, and when the user exits the texts will be returned to the invoice verification function to continue.

Within configuration, you indicate via flags if you wish to use this function, and then you must indicate which texts should be displayed. See Chapter 4 for the details of configuring this function.

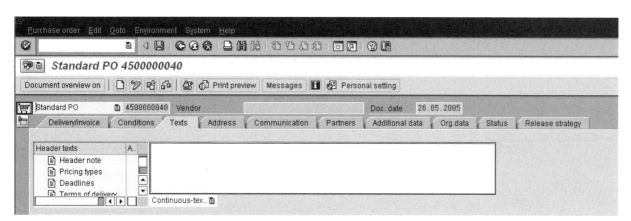

Figure 2.25 Purchase-Order Header Texts

If text is not keyed into a notifiable text window on the purchase order, then no window will be displayed at the invoice stage. The window only appears if text has been entered in a notifiable text.

An Example of How to Use this Function

To use this function, you need to do the following:

▶ Decide if you wish this option to be used in your organization. If so, then switch it on in configuration (See Chapter 4).

▶ Decide which purchase order header text or texts should be highlighted to the user when an invoice is being posted.

▶ One tip here is to get your materials-management consultant to configure an extra text element on the purchase-order header, specifically designed to hold invoice-relevant notes. However, you can simply choose to use existing text elements if you wish. The advantage to creating a new element is that it can be named "invoice verification text," so it will be obvious to the user that this will be seen by the invoice department when an invoice is keyed.

It is not always obvious why you may need to highlight a message to the invoice-verification clerk, but consider the following situation.

Invoice verification works on the principle of three-way matching. So, if the vendor sends in an invoice that matches the quantity delivered at the price on the purchase order, then that vendor will be paid at the appropriate time, automatically.

There are occasions where you may not want the vendor to be paid automatically, even though the three-way match process indicates that al is well.

What if the purchase order is for multiple items, and you only want to pay for these when all of them have been received, because they are no use to you until you have everything from the vendor? If the vendor was to just send part of this order and then invoice for the same part of the order, the invoice would normally match and be paid even though you are left without those vital items that you need in order to use the items you already have received. This is where the notifiable texts can help.

When the purchase order is raised, the header text "invoice verification text" is entered, stating something like: "This purchase order should only be paid when ALL items have been received; accept no partial invoices from the vendor."

Then, when the partial invoice is entered, the user will get a pop-up window informing him or her that there are relevant texts that should be read before continuing.

When the text is viewed, the user can then check to see if this is a full invoice (by examining the purchase-order items proposed by the system).

This text notification can provide functionality that at first appears to be lacking. It is well worth discussing with the main financial users to determine how relevant it is to their requirements. This functionality is often not implemented because it has not been requested, and it is often not requested because the user (and sometimes even the consultant) does not know that it is available.

2.10 Summary

This chapter introduced the main elements of invoice verification. When used to their full capabilities, these options should provide you with an efficient and beneficial process. Chapter 3 will focus on the financial elements, and Chapter 4 will show you how to configure the various functions mentioned in this chapter.

3 Financial Aspects of Invoice Verification

This chapter covers the financial elements of invoice verification. As discussed earlier, the invoice-verification function is normally designed and configured by the materials-management team in close coordination with the finance team. Therefore, this chapter deliberately avoids detailed financial terminology and describes the processes in basic terms.

3.1 Overview

The invoice-verification function is designed to capture the details from the vendor's invoice and match them against expected quantities and values. The financial postings of a matched invoice are essentially the same as those of an unmatched invoice.

The only difference is that a blocking flag set with the unmatched invoice will prevent payment to the vendor until the invoice has been matched or cleared for payment.

Postings involve the following:

▶ Vendor account
▶ Tax accounts where appropriate
▶ Price variance accounts
▶ Goods-receipt/invoice-receipt clearing account
▶ Stock accounts (mainly for price corrections caused by the invoice).

Other accounts, such as freight, customs, or duty may be involved depending on the circumstances. The accounts that will be posted are determined automatically by the system, according to basic accounting rules and procedures.

3.2 Automatic Account Determination

A complex configuration step must be set up correctly in order to point the various postings involved to the correct general-ledger accounts.

This function is used in two different ways, although it is essentially the same configuration step. These two ways are:

▶ Setting up the automatic account determination. This is used for the majority of the materials-management postings such as receipts, issues, or write-offs.
▶ Setting up the postings made during invoice verification. This is the same transaction, but a flag switches it between normal materials-management postings and those involved in invoice verification.

It is important to realize that what is being configured is the number of the general-ledger account that should be used in various standard accounts postings. You are not affecting the way that invoice verification accounts for the postings involved; this is built into the system and should not be altered. You are merely attaching the number of the account that you want to be posted to in a number of scenarios.

The process is covered in Section 4.3. It should be carried out by the materials-management team and the finance team working together. The materials-management team should be describing the various scenarios in invoice verification, and the finance team should be determining the correct general ledger for each scenario.

3.3 The Goods Received/Invoice Received Clearing Account

This special clearing account essentially gives details of the balance of non-invoiced receipts and/or invoices received for items not yet received.

The total value in the account indicates the amount of funds you need to have available in order to pay for the items you have received but have not yet paid for.

It is more relevant to quantities than values, and this affects the way that it values any postings made. It has to clear the full value when the quantity invoiced matches the quantity received, regardless of the values involved. For example, an invoice for 10 items at a value of €100 will clear a goods receipt of 10 items of any value (the same, higher, or lower) as long as the receipt relates to the same item on the same purchase order.

If there are entries in the account that have not cleared automatically, this indicates that you have either received invoices for items you have not yet received or you have items that you have received that have not yet been invoiced. A goods receipt/invoice receipt clearing account with many unresolved entries normally indicates that the processes designed for invoice verification are less than ideal. This often happens when the GR-Based IV flag has been used inappropriately (see Section 2.1).

Sample Scenarios of the Use of the GR/IR Clearing Account

The use of the clearing account can be more easily understood with the following examples.

▶ **GR/IR Clearing Sample Scenario One**:

1. A purchase order is sent to the Vendor for 100 items at €1 each.
2. The vendor sends a partial delivery of 50 pieces.
3. Upon receipt, a posting is made of €50 to the stock account for the 50 pieces received, and a balancing entry of €50 (negative) is posted to the GR/IR clearing account. The transaction therefore balances.
4. The GR/IR clearing account now shows that there is a need to keep €50 available to pay an invoice that is likely to arrive in the near future for the 50 pieces received.
5. The vendor then sends in an invoice for €50 for the 50 pieces that were delivered.

6. When the invoice is entered, it will post a balancing entry of 50 pieces at the goods-receipt value (€50) to the GR/IR clearing account, regardless of the invoice value. This clears the account.
7. €50 were posted to the clearing account with the opposing €50 (negative) being posted to the vendor account as a debt to be paid.
8. The end result is a zero balance on the GR/IR clearing account indicating that all receipts now have been paid for.

▶ **GR/IR Clearing Sample Scenario Two**:

1. A purchase order is sent to the Vendor for 100 items at €1 each.
2. The vendor sends a partial delivery of 50 pieces.
3. Upon receipt, a posting is made of €50 to the stock account for the 50 pieces received and a balancing entry of €50 (negative) is posted to the GR/IR clearing account and the transaction therefore balances.
4. The GR/IR clearing account now shows that there is a need to keep €50 available to pay for an invoice that is likely to arrive in the near future for the 50 pieces received. To this point this is the same as in Scenario One.
5. This time the vendor sends in an invoice for €100 for 100 pieces (the full amount, even though only half of the order has been received).
6. When the invoice is entered, it will post an entry of 100 pieces totaling €100 (based on the goods receipt value of €1 each) to the clearing account. The invoice will be blocked from payment because the remaining 50 pieces have not yet been received.
7. The end result of the invoice entry is a balance of €50 for 50 items on the GR/IR clearing account, and this will remain there until we receive the remaining 50 pieces (or manually balance this by using a special clearing entry). The clearing account therefore indicates that we have paid for some materials that we have not yet received.

▶ **GR/IR Clearing Sample Scenario Three**:

1. A purchase order is sent to the Vendor for 100 items at €1 each.
2. The vendor sends the first 50 pieces.

3. Upon receipt, a posting of €50 is made to the stock account for the 50 pieces received, and a balancing entry of €50 (negative) is posted to the GR/IR clearing account. The transaction therefore balances.

4. The GR/IR clearing account now shows that there is a need to keep €50 available to pay for an invoice that is likely to arrive in the near future for the 50 pieces received. To this point, the situation is the same as in Scenario One.

5. The vendor sends an invoice for €25 for 25 pieces (this is less than the delivered amount), and this may be an error by the vendor.

6. When the invoice is entered, it will post a balancing entry of 25 pieces at the GR value (regardless of the invoice value) of €25. The invoice will be cleared for payment because it is for less than the value that we owe the vendor.

7. The end result is a balance of €25 (negative) for 25 items on the GR/IR account. This will remain there until we receive an invoice for the remaining 25 pieces.

▶ **GR/IR Clearing Sample Scenario Four**:

1. A purchase order is sent to the vendor for 100 items at €1 each.

2. The vendor sends the first 50 pieces.

3. Upon receipt, a posting of €50 is made to the stock account for the 50 pieces received, and a balancing entry of €50 (negative) is posted to the GR/IR clearing account. The transaction therefore balances.

4. The GR/IR clearing account now shows that we need to keep €50 available to pay for an invoice that is likely to arrive in the near future for the 50 pieces received. So far, this is the same as in Scenario One.

5. The vendor sends an invoice for €75 for 50 pieces. Again, this may be an error by the vendor.

6. When we enter the invoice, it will post a balancing entry of 50 pieces at the GR value (regardless of the invoice value) of €50 to the clearing account. The invoice will be blocked for payment because of the price difference.

7. The end result is a zero balance on the GR/IR account even though the vendor has charged more than we expected. The reason: We were expecting an invoice

for 50 pieces, and we now have an invoice for 50 pieces, so there is no balance to account for.

Using MR11 to Manage the GR/IR Clearing Account

Transaction MR11 is designed to be used to view and/ or maintain the GR/IR clearing account. This function is normally the responsibility of the finance department, but there must be assistance from the purchasing and inventory departments to determine whether the balance should be cleared or left for future action (such as a goods receipt or credit note). Figure 3.1 shows the initial selection screen.

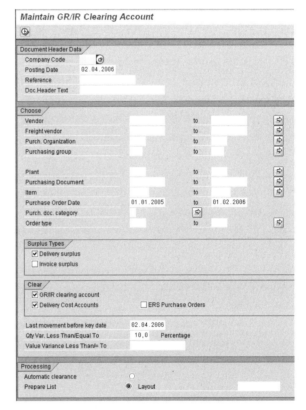

Figure 3.1 MR11 Selection Screen for GR/IR Clearing Account

This transaction is used for two main purposes. These are:

▶ As a report to show the current situation

▶ As a clearing transaction to balance out the entries and tidy up the discrepancies

Use the main selection options in the **Document Header Data** and **Choose** sections to narrow down the entries to only those that you wish to deal with. Many of the options available in the other fields on the selection screen have very specific uses.

The clearing account is designed to show the value of non-invoiced receipts or invoices with no receipts. The selection options therefore include the flags to show either or both of these alternatives, which are shown in Figure 3.1 in the **Surplus Types** section.

If you select **Delivery surplus,** you will only see those deliveries (i.e., receipts) that have not yet been invoiced. If you select **Invoice surplus,** you will only see those invoices for which a full receipt has not yet been posted. You can select both flags if you wish. This is ideal when you want to see the total balance of the account.

The **Clear** window indicates which clearing accounts you wish to work with. You can choose the **GR/IR**, **Freight**, or **ERS clearing accounts** with these flags.

The final three fields at the bottom of the **Choose** section allow you to control the records to be displayed, depending on the size of the imbalance. This setting can be used to clear old records that are for small variances.

These small variances could take a lot of effort to clear for little benefit. If the difference is very small and also very old, you can normally assume that it can be cleared automatically. For instance, if an invoice was received six months ago for bulk materials, and the invoice quantity was for 9.875 tons, and the goods receipt was posted for 9.800 tons, then it would be safe to assume that the vendor is unlikely to deliver the missing 0.075 of a ton six months later.

You can use these settings to indicate the age of the items and the allowed variances that you want to view or to clear automatically. Let's look at examples of the entries made to the three fields.

▶ The **Last movement before key date** field could be set to a date six months earlier. This means that the system will not consider anything that has had an invoice, credit memo, or receipt posted in the last six months. This way, you can assume that the purchase order and invoice are to be classed as fully processed.

▶ The **Qty Var. Less Than/Equal To** field is used to limit the size of item to be cleared. Set this at a very low percentage initially, and then increase it gradually for each run, so that you can be sure that the records being cleared are only small differences. An initial setting of 2% to start with, rising to 10%, is

normal. But the percentage used should be in line with the **Last movement before key date** field. This is important, because a small percentage on an invoice posted six months ago may be cleared without major risk, but the same percentage on an invoice posted only last month may be premature.

▶ The **Value Variance Less Than/= To** field is used in conjunction with the percentage to ensure that you do not clear large values just because they are a small percentage of a high-value invoice.

Note: If you just want to view all entries in the clearing account, enter maximum percentages and values in these fields and ensure that the purchase order dates, etc., are broad enough to capture the required entries.

The **Processing** window controls whether the transaction is being run as a report or an update. The **Prepare list** flag must always be set "on" if you just want to view the entries. Setting the **Automatic clearance** flag on will clear all entries that match the selection criteria (taking the percentages and values into consideration).

Regular Maintenance of the Clearing Account

The clearing account should be maintained regularly, at least monthly. If it is not, the contents of the account become unmanageable.

I recommend running the automatic clearing with a date of six or so months ago, for a percentage of 5% to 10% and a value of less than €20. This should clear all of the simple variances that are not worth investigating.

Once this is done, you should run the transaction again but this time as a report. You then can investigate any suspicious entries and either chase the receipt of the stock or invoice (whichever is overdue) or manually clear the entry if appropriate. You can clear manually by selecting the record and clicking on the save icon, as shown in Figure 3.2.

The overall result of a clearing, whether done manually or automatically, is to indicate that the outstanding invoice or receipt is not likely to happen. The system will then base its financial postings on the quantity and value invoiced so far (if any) being used to value the receipt that has been posted (if any).

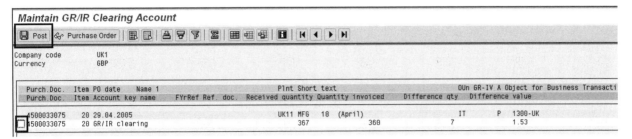

Figure 3.2 Detailed Display of MR11

If there has been a receipt of 100 items at €10, each, for example, the stock account has been updated with a value of €1,000 when the receipt was posted. If the invoice is received but the quantity invoiced was 90 and the difference is cleared with MR11, then there will be a posting of a negative value of €100 to the stock account if the item is Moving Average Price (MAP) controlled. There will be posting to a price-variance account if the item is standard-price controlled. This occurs because this is now the true cost of the items received.

The clearing values are stored on the clearing document for enquiry and audit-trail purposes. Everything balances, and this entry is cleared.

The GR/IR clearing account can often become more complicated than it needs to be. This can happen if invoices are being posted against the wrong purchase orders. Worse still, a purchase order may have been created deliberately to match an invoice that has been received, where there was already a purchase order but it was not used because it couldn't be traced. This results in a purchase order (the original one) being left on the clearing account with no invoice to clear it against.

In such a case, you should reverse the purchase order that was specially created to match the invoice and then rematch with the correct one. You do have the option of just clearing the original order using MR11. While this might appear to work, you will have had two receipts posted, both with a value, and so your financial postings are now incorrect.

Note: It is always worth the effort to trace a purchase order to match against the invoice, as this will ensure that the clearing account is not corrupted. Do not allow purchase orders to be created just to match

against invoices unless this is a controlled part of your standard process.

3.4 Tax Processing Within Invoice Verification

Different countries have different tax rules and procedures, and so you need to ensure that your company codes have been assigned to the correct tax procedures when they were configured. In general, this is a procedure such as TAXGB for taxes in Great Britain. This will allow appropriate tax codes to be maintained with the correct percentages. These are:

▶ V1—VAT at 17.5%
▶ V0—VAT at 0%

These codes can be entered on the purchase-order item line (**Invoice** tab), as shown in Figure 3.3.

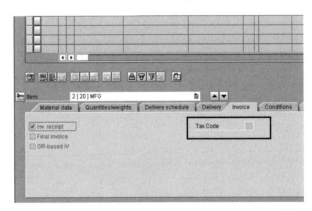

Figure 3.3 Tax Code Field on Purchase Order Item (Invoice Tab)

This entry is not mandatory (except for ERS orders, described in Section 2.4). This means that the VAT code may be blank on the purchase-order item line in the MIRO invoice-verification screen, and so you will need to specify the relevant code or, at the very least, set up default codes in configuration (see Section 4.5). The tax code can also be specified on the **Basic data** tab of the MIRO transaction, or it can be left blank, especially if multiple codes exist on the purchase order. This code applies to the invoice as a whole. Figure 3.4 shows the tax-code field on the MIRO **Basic data** tab.

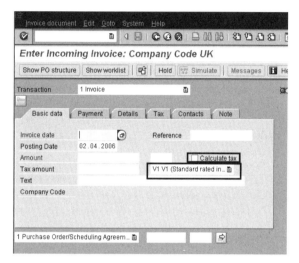

Figure 3.4 Tax Code Field on MIRO Basic Data Tab

Note: If you need to use different tax codes for the same item on a purchase order, always have a different order-item line for each tax code. Within MIRO, you cannot have the same order-item line repeated in the line-item display. Thus, you will not be able to specify two different tax codes for the same item.

The Calculate Tax Flag

You have the option of flagging the **Calculate tax** box to indicate that you want the system to calculate the tax that applies to this invoice. This is shown in Figure 3.4.

Note: The **Amount** field on the same tab must always include any taxes. The tax amount field should contain the portion of the total invoice amount that is tax. Alternatively, you should set the **Calculate tax** flag to have this calculated automatically based on the tax codes specified.

There is no right or wrong setting of the **Calculate tax** flag; the end result is the same either way. However, I

recommend that you normally enter the tax amount manually where possible. By doing this, you enable the system to check the tax calculation from the vendor. If you merely flag the **Calculate tax** box each time, you may miss the fact that the vendor's calculations are different. This may occur because the **Manage small differences** tolerance settings are accepting the small rounding errors each time.

By manually keying the tax amount specified by the vendor, you are fully checking the invoice and tax amounts. For example, if the vendor undercharged you by a small amount for the items on the invoice and somehow managed to overcharge you for the tax by the same amount, you need to capture this information. If you have the **Calculate tax** flag set on, the invoice would balance and it shouldn't. With the flag set off, the system will highlight the price differences and the incorrect tax calculation.

The Tax Tab in the MIRO Transaction

If you select the tax tab within the MIRO transaction, you will be able to see and/or maintain the different tax codes that are relevant to this invoice and the tax values against each code. This is especially useful if you have an invoice with multiple tax codes. Figure 3.5 shows the detail available on the tax tab

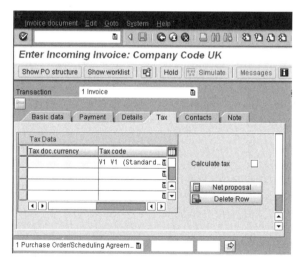

Figure 3.5 Tax Tab Details

You can change the **Calculate tax** field in this tab if required. You can enter, delete or change values against each tax code, and you can view the effect on the tax values of posting the invoice net (i.e., net of cash discounts, covered in Section 4.5), by clicking on the **Net proposal** button.

3.5 Moving Average Price/Standard Price

The price control (on the **Accounting** view of the material master record) is an important setting and can dramatically influence the way that values in goods receipts and invoice receipts are posted. You can use different methods for different materials, or you can decide to have the same price control used for all materials. Which option to use is often decided by a personal preference within the finance department, based on previous experience, but it can also depend on how variable your purchase prices are.

If your prices are relatively static and predictable, then standard pricing can sometimes be more appropriate. This is because there are fewer postings to the price-variance account, and so there are fewer corrections to manage.

MAP control tends to be more appropriate if the purchase prices vary more frequently. In such cases, fewer price variances will be posted, and the MAP is more likely to reflect the true costs of the items because all costs are posted to the stock account. In contrast, standard-price-controlled materials only post the standard price to the stock account.

It is important to realize that values are sometimes posted to the stock account when an invoice is posted. This only happens if you are using the MAP control and when the invoice values cause adjustments due to different prices or because additional costs—such as delivery costs—are entered at invoice stage.

The Difference Between Standard Pricing and MAP

There is one main difference between the two options. With standard pricing, any posting to or from the stock account will always be at the standard price regardless of the actual values involved. With MAP, all values that can be attributed to the cost of the item will be posted to the stock account. The price is then averaged out against the value of existing stock, and when an item is issued it will always be at the relevant MAP.

Advantages of Each Option

Which option is best depends on many factors, and what is classed as an advantage by one person could be seen as a disadvantage by another.

For example, one perceived advantage of standard pricing is that the value used at consumption or goods-issue stage remains constant, and this can help with budgeting, as every department will have the same costs associated with consumption.

On the other hand, the standard price is sometimes only set once or twice a year and so it is unlikely to be correct all year long, especially if the prices vary throughout the year. This situation may result in every posting being at an incorrect value, so that the profit and loss data on the movements of these items is likely to be misleading.

The differences caused by this will be stored in a price-variance account, and this will need to be managed so that the actual costs are reflected correctly in the profit and loss statements,

If you use MAP, one perceived advantage is that the consumption values will be based on an average of the actual costs of the material, and so they are more likely to be a fair assumption of cost. But if two items are consumed at different dates and therefore at potentially two different values, is it fair that one posting could be at a very different cost to another for exactly the same material? If two different departments are using the same materials for similar purposes and are being charged at different prices, at least one may feel that this is unfair.

Let's look at this example which illustrates the main differences between the two options and shows some of the advantages and disadvantages of each option.

▶ We start with two items in stock, one purchased at a cost of €100 (perhaps part of a special deal) and the other for €500 (perhaps it was purchased from a different and more expensive vendor for some reason). The production department wants to use one of the items as a component.

▶ If MAP control is used, the MAP would be set by the system at €300 (100 plus 500, divided by two) and there would be €600 in the stock account. The €300 MAP could be seen to be a reasonable cost price to use, even though we have never actually purchased one of these items at €300. The production planning department will be charged €300, and if anyone else was to use the remaining item they too would be charged €300. The total cost to purchase has therefore been passed on to the departments that have used the items.

▶ If standard price control is used, the standard price will have been set manually (for the sake of this example) at €200, probably because it was believed that this would be a reasonable price to pay for this item. The stock account would contain only €400 in total, (the receipts, as with every posting, were at the standard price regardless of the purchase costs). The first receipt would have posted a negative €100 to the price-variance account and €200 (the standard price) to the stock account (a total of €100 to match the actual costs). The second receipt would have posted a positive €300 to the price variance account and €200 (the standard price) to the stock account (a total of €500 to match the actual costs).

▶ The production department would be charged €200, and if anyone else was to use the other item they too would be charged €200. The stock account would now be zero (as it was with the MAP option), but the total charged for the use of the items is only €400. There is still €200 in the price variance account (the negative €100 for the first receipt and the €300 from the second receipt).

Both options use accepted financial postings, and so the choice depends on which is most appropriate for the situation involved.

Although the above example focuses on the postings caused by goods receipts and issues, the concept is the same during invoice verification. In this case, if there are any postings that affect stock accounts, the system will use the above rules to determine whether that posting should be made directly to or from the stock account (for MAP materials) or to or from the price-variance account (for standard-priced materials).

3.6   The Payment Run

This process can be automated, but many businesses prefer to retain manual control over what gets paid and when. Payment run is a standard SAP transaction that works on

line or scheduled as a batch job. The transaction is called F110, or you can use transaction F110S to schedule the payment run at set intervals. Figure 3.6 shows the initial screen of F110 and the tabs that are available.

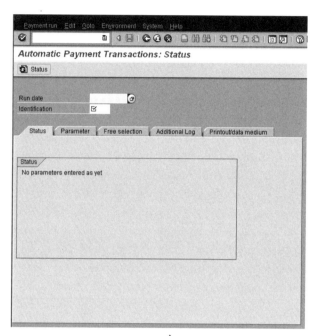

Figure 3.6 Initial Screen of Transaction F110, the Payment Run

The initial screen is used to give the payment run a unique reference and to capture the payment-run date. Indicate the date of the payment run and specify an identification code (up to five characters). This code will be used to identify the result of the run later. Fill out the remainder of the selections on the four tabs available.

The Parameter Tab

The parameter tab section is used to control which items are paid. It enables you to select certain company codes, payment methods, vendors, and/or customers. In implementations that use multiple companies, each company can still control when, and who they pay. Figure 3.7 shows the **Parameter** tab fields.

You select the company code or codes that you wish to include in the payment run. If you are entering more than one company code, enter each code followed by a comma and then the next company code (no spaces). You can enter a range or ranges of company codes by using the format 0001, 0006, which in this case indicates all company codes from 0001 to 0006 inclusive.

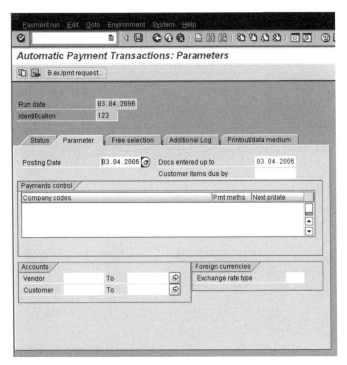

Figure 3.7 Parameter Tab Fields

Indicate the payment methods you want to process (check, BACS, etc.) by entering the single letter code or codes, again without spaces, but this time with no commas. Note that all documents that match the selections made will be included in the payment run. If a document has a payment method that is not included here, it will not be paid, and it will appear in the list of exceptions.

You must enter the date of the next payment run so that the program can select the correct payments to make. This field ensures that you pay your vendors at the latest possible moment without losing discounts and without missing deadlines. The program simply uses this date to determine whether any deadline for payment (or discount) will be missed if the payment is left until the next payment run. This means that you can run the payment program regularly without paying too early. It is recommended to run the payment program frequently so that dates are not missed.

Running the program infrequently will also result in payments being made too early. Here are some examples:

▶ If you only run the payment program once every month, and a vendor gives you 14 days to pay, the invoice will be paid early. The reason: It will be paid in the current run because if it isn't, the next payment run will be too late. In fact, the payment will be made up to 14 days early depending on the date of the run.

▶ If you run the payment program weekly (or even daily), you are less likely to pay an invoice early, because the program will determine that there is another chance to pay the invoice later and so it can wait until a future payment run.

▶ If you decide to run the payment program infrequently, then you may need to trick the system into thinking that the next payment run will be earlier than it is by entering a date for the next run as early as the next day. This will prevent items from being paid early, but you will miss deadlines for payment for many items.

Enter a range or list of vendors or customers you want to include in the payment run. Use the range 1 to ZZZZZZZZZZ if you wish to include all partners.

Enter an exchange rate type if you do not wish to use the default average rate (rate type **M**).

The Free Selection Tab

The free selection tab provides you with a flexible range of fields that can be used to include or exclude items due for payment. This is especially useful if you need to use specific fields on the Document, Vendor, or Customer. Figure 3.8 shows the **Free Selection** tab fields.

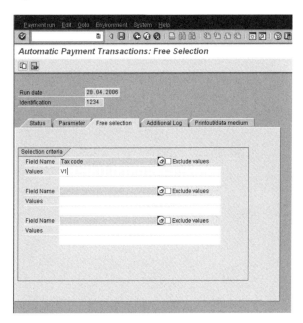

Figure 3.8 Free Selection Tab Fields

You can enter values for selected fields that you wish to include or exclude in the run.

Select the source of the required field (**Document**, **Vendor**, or **Customer**) from the pull-down list, select the appropriate field from the list displayed, then enter the values and or ranges to be excluded or included (depending on the **Exclude values** flag).

The Additional Log tab

This is not relevant to payment runs in an established SAP system. It is only used in the early days of an implementation when full payment logs are required just to verify what has happened in full detail. This detail is normally not required or adds no value once the payment worked as expected. Figure 3.9 shows the **Additional Log** tab fields.

This tab is normally left blank during payment runs. It can be used in early or test runs to provide a log of the actions that took place during the run. You can decide what you want to see in this log by selecting the appro-

priate flags and indicating any specific vendors or customers.

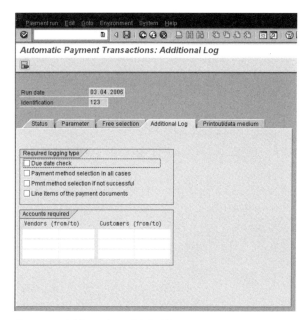

Figure 3.9 Additional Log Tab Fields

The Printout/data medium tab

Figure 3.10 shows the Printout/data medium tab fields.

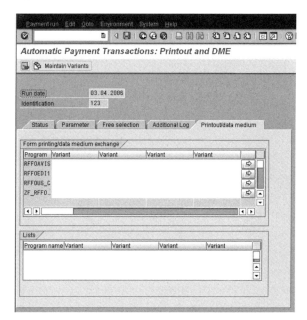

Figure 3.10 Printout/Data Medium Tab Fields

You can indicate the variant to be used for the appropriate print program for payment documents and other items. You can also select the list and variant to be used for the log and summary reports.

Running F110

To execute the payment run with transaction F110, you must save the entries first. I advise saving different variants for each run so you don't to enter all details each time. When you have saved the details, the status screen will be displayed.

You can then either run the transaction as a full payment run or as a proposal run, in order to calculate who will be paid and what the total value will be without actually making payment. When the program is executed, you can view the progress from the status tab, it will show the status as each stage is completed.

The F110S Transaction

This has the same fields and options as the F110 transaction but is designed to be used when scheduling the payment run as a batch job. All the fields are on one screen and can be saved as a variant. Make sure that you set the **Proposal** flag if you wish to just see the proposed payments rather than a full payment run. Figure 3.11 shows the transaction F110S screen.

3.7 Summary

Although this chapter focuses on the financial aspects of invoice verification, this process should not be handled by the financial team alone. The materials-management team must be involved in the financial design. Some implementations miss this vital point, and the result is a function that operates correctly from a financial point of view but does not operate efficiently or simply from a user viewpoint.

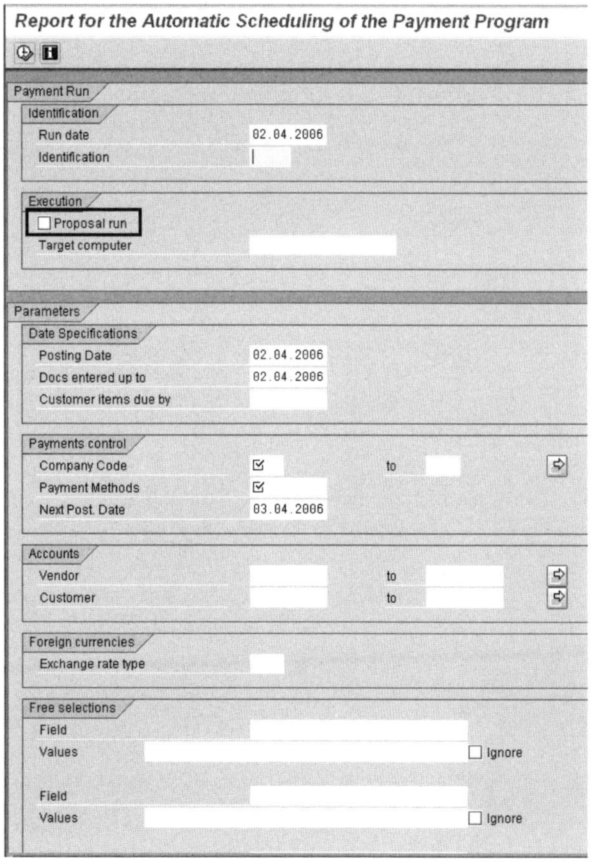

Figure 3.11 Transaction F110S Screen

4 Configuration

This chapter covers the configuration options available within SAP Invoice Verification. This is not merely a case of knowing what to configure. It is vitally important to know the effects of the many configuration options. Some options are quite simple, and the settings are obvious. Others sometimes appear unimportant or irrelevant, and yet they can sometimes make a huge difference to the functionality available. This chapter will focus largely on the less obvious areas of configuration.

I strongly recommend that you read the ample text help that SAP provides on each configuration step. The help-text icon is found on each configuration menu option, as shown in Figure 4.1.

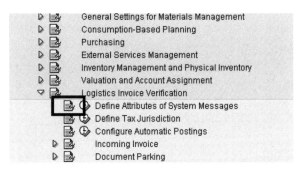

Figure 4.1 SAP Configuration Help Text Icon

With a few exceptions, this help text is normally very useful, and it can sometimes help just by confirming what you already believed about the configuration step for which it was meant to be used.

Although every step is covered within this chapter, extra time will be spent on the more complex options and in particular on those that can unlock extra functionality. By following this guide and confirming your assumptions with the help text available, you should be able to tackle the configuration of Invoice Verification with confidence and provide the users with a flexible, efficient, and user-friendly process.

4.1 Basic Configuration.

I recommend carrying out the configuration via the main transaction SPRO. There are individual transactions for many configuration options, but by using these you can sometimes miss out on additional options that are available. By using SPRO and drilling down through the menus, you will follow the basic configuration in the sequence that SAP recommends. In addition, you will be able to view the help documentation at each level.

The SPRO transaction will look similar to that shown in Figure 4.2, depending on which version of SAP you are using.

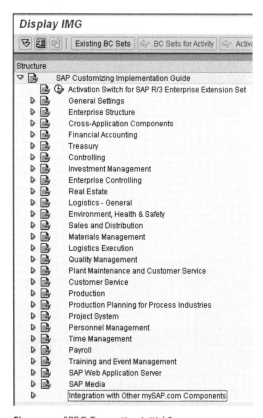

Figure 4.2 SPRO Transaction Initial Screen

In all the following examples, we assume that you will use the **SAP Reference Implementation Guide (IMG) option.** This option shows all of the configuration steps. If your implementation is using IMG Projects, then you may need to select the appropriate project from the list. The options available within a project IMG are normally restricted to those relevant to the implementation. Thus, by using the SAP Reference IMG at this point, every option will be included.

Figure 4.3 shows the expanded configuration menu. It is worth noting that invoice verification is referred to as Logistics Invoice Verification. You will find this within the Materials Management configuration menu (not the Financial Accounting menu as you might expect).

Note that the invoice-verification configuration is split down into several sections. The standard SAP approach is to have the structure of the menus set up so that you start at the top and work your way down. This is only a very rough guide. As you can see from the sequence here—starting with **Define Attributes of System Messages** as the first option—it is not a hard and fast rule. Each of the configuration options will be covered in the sequence they appear in the standard SAP menu list for invoice verification, shown in Figure 4.3.

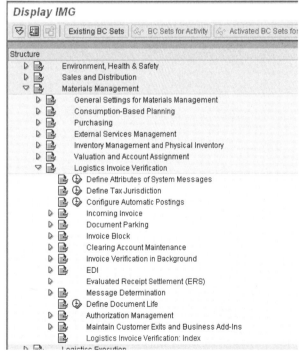

Figure 4.3 Standard SAP Menu List for Invoice Verification

The first three menu options—**Define Attributes of System Messages**, **Define Tax Jurisdiction**, and **Configure Automatic Postings**—are not sub-menus, as such; they are single configuration steps. They do not affect a specific area in invoice verification, but are more general and so are not contained within the more specific sub-menus.

4.2 Define the Attributes of System Messages

This is a powerful configuration option, and yet many implementations overlook its benefits. It can be used to control many of the messages that are displayed during invoice verification. A message can be set as an error message to stop any further processing. It also can be set as a warning message and so allow the user to continue, or it can be set off so that the message is not displayed.

However, switching off a message in this manner does not always work. Some errors cannot be switched off because the program logic would not be able to continue without the error being corrected. The fact that you can configure the message to be off does not mean it will not be set to an error by the program. Apart from these exceptions, setting the messages to error and warnings according to your needs is often essential.

There is an additional control that can be a real benefit and that is the ability to control individual messages by **User Name**. This can result in one user getting an error message and being prevented from continuing while another user being gets a warning message and is allowed to continue.

This capability can be useful when you want certain messages to prevent a standard user from continuing—for instance when a large change is made to the Moving Average Price (MAP)—but you want the supervisor to be able to process the invoice if need be. If you were to merely set the error message to stop further processing, then nobody could continue. But by setting the message as an error message for all standard users and then setting it as a warning message for the supervisor or supervisors, you achieve flexibility in processing.

You also may need to set messages differently for batch runs than you do for online runs of the same transaction. Often there is little point in having any warning messages in the batch run because the update will need to continue anyway.

Moreover, you may wish to set messages that are normally warnings to full error messages to stop the batch run, because you have no way of making a decision based on that message. Whatever the reason, being able to set different types of messages for batch runs is often essential.

How to Configure System Messages

If you want to have all of the standard messages unchanged, then you need do nothing. If you leave the table empty, the standard defaults for each message will be used.

If you want to control a message, you will need to find the relevant message number. This can be obtained from the pull-down list of the message number field, as shown in Figure 4.4, or by double-clicking on any message when it is displayed.

You add the selected message as a new entry by clicking on the **New Entries** icon and entering, or by selecting the appropriate message number; the message text and the standard settings will be filled in when you press enter.

You then can change the flags. If you leave the **User Name** field blank, these settings will apply to all users. If you need different settings for different users, then you need to have a separate entry for each.

Remember: If the standard message setting is to be used for some users, then you only need entries for the users who will have a non-standard setting, because the table should contain only the exceptions from the standard settings. If the standard setting for a message is an error, and you want a supervisor to be allowed to continue if he or she gets this message, then you only need to have one entry in the table with the supervisor's user name and the flag set to a warning message. Figure 4.5 shows an example of message settings.

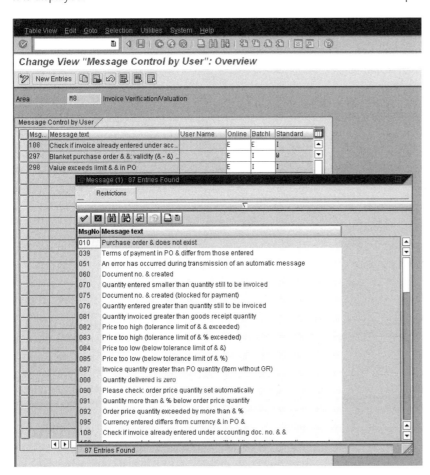

Figure 4.4 List of Messages from Pull-Down Option of Message Field

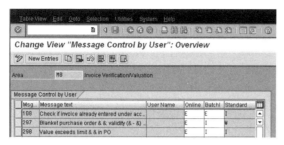

Figure 4.5 Three messages Being Controlled

The effects of the settings on the three entries shown in the example in Figure 4.5 are as follows:

▶ Message 108 is normally set as an "information" message. It is not a warning, merely a message to inform the user of an event (it has an **I** in the **Standard** field). If this message is triggered in a batch job, then it will be treated as a serious error and the record will not be updated (it has an **E** in the **Batchl** field). If the message is triggered online, then it will have the standard information message (it has an **I** in the **Online** field). This message will be given the same setting for all users (the **User Name** field is blank).

▶ Message 297 is normally set as a warning message: The user will see a warning but will be allowed to continue (it has an **W** in the **Standard** field). If this message is triggered in a batch job, then it will be treated as an information message, and the record can be processed if the batch run allows this (it has an **I** in the **Batchl** field). If the message is triggered online, then the user will see an error message and will not be allowed to continue until the error has been resolved (it has an **E** in the **Online** field). This message will be given the same setting for all users (the **User Name** field is blank).

▶ Message 298 normally is set as an information message (it has an **I** in the Standard field). If this message is triggered in a batch job, then it will again issue an information message (it has an **I** in the **Batchl** field). If the message is triggered online then it will have the standard information message (it has an **I** in the **Online** field). This message will be given the same setting for all users (the **User Name** field is blank).

It is normal to start with this table empty during the initial phases of design and only add entries as the design begins to take shape.

4.3 Define Tax Jurisdiction

You can be forgiven for thinking that there is a bug in the IMG when you first examine this configuration option. It is entitled **Define tax jurisdiction,** and yet when you open it you are taken to the configuration of plants.

This is not a bug. It is just that there is a setting on the configuration of plants that contains the tax-jurisdiction data, and so this uses the same transaction.

You may not need to configure this data, because this configuration is designed for use in the United States only.

Select the **Plant** from the list and click on the **Details** icon (or double click on the **Plant** line). This will take you to the plant-details screen shown in Figure 4.6.

This field should always be set to the city where goods are supplied. This may be different from the address stored for the plant.

4.4 Configure Automatic Postings

The most important thing to realize about this configuration option is that you are not configuring the way the system carries out the accounting. You are merely specifying the general-ledger (G/L) account numbers of the accounts that the system should use in specific predefined circumstances.

You can change the way that the system carries out its accounting processes to some extent, but this is rarely required and certainly not recommended.

The system has validated standard built-in accounting practices that are designed to match the rigid rules of accounting. Any changes to this could lead to problems. All you normally need to do is to specify the account numbers to be used for certain transactions such as Goods receipt/Invoice receipt (GR/IR) clearing, price variances, and freight provisions.

A combined team of materials-management and finance staff normally carries out this configuration. Sometimes it is left to one or the other of these groups, with a less-than-optimal result. The materials-management team is normally responsible for the configuration of invoice verification, but team members often feel unqualified to make the financial decisions involved in this step.

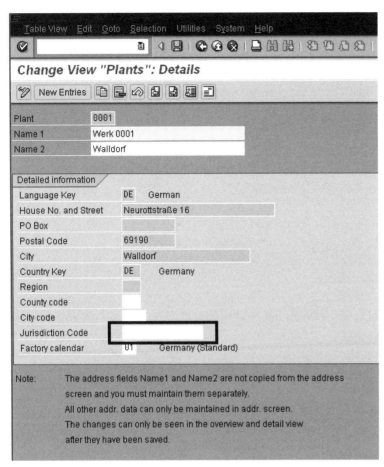

Figure 4.6 Plant Details Screen Showing the Jurisdiction Field

However, if the process is merely handed over to the finance team, these people will not normally have been involved in the full invoice-verification design, including the detailed processes that surround price variances, freight, and similar transactions. So a combined team effort is the way to go. There are three main sections within the configuration option:

▶ Account assignment
▶ Simulation
▶ G/L accounts

Each section is very different, so we should think of these as being three separate configuration transactions. In fact, of the three, only the account-assignment option allows you to configure anything, the other two options are display transactions that can be used to help ensure that the settings are correct.

Account Assignment

This is the main configuration step in automatic account determination and is probably the most complex configuration of all in SAP. The terminology used does nothing to help simplify the process. The word "valuation" is used in many of the main entities involved (valuation area, valuation area group, valuation class, valuation modifier, etc.), and this adds to the confusion. A quick explanation of the main terminology is essential before we dig into the details and so the main terms are explained below. These are:

▶ The valuation area, in almost all stock-based implementations, is simply the financial name for a plant. This means that in this case, whenever the term "valuation area" is used, you can safely substitute the word "plant" for it. In exceptional circumstances, the valuation area can be set to be the same as the company code, but this means that plants cannot be accounted for differently, because the company code is a level above the plant level.

▶ The valuation Area group allows you to group similar plants together to remove the need to duplicate entries that apply across all plants. Typical groups include all production facilities in one group, all warehouses in another, and non-stock plants in a final group. You also sometimes can find all plants grouped into one single valuation-area group.

▶ The valuation class is also a grouping function. It allows materials that are to be treated the same, for accounting purposes, to be grouped together. Typical valuation classes reflect the types of materials involved such as raw materials, finished products, or services. They often relate in some way to the material types but this is not a requirement. Basically it allows you to set automatic accounting by group, i.e. valuation class, rather than for each individual material.

▶ The valuation class is stored on the material master record (**Accounting** view), and possible entries are controlled by material type configuration. Figure 4.7 shows the **Valuation Class** field on the material master Accounting view.

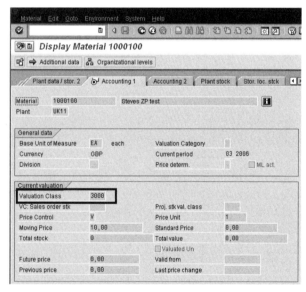

Figure 4.7 Valuation Class Field on Material Master Accounting View

The **transaction/event key** presents the biggest challenge to understanding the automatic- accounting terminology.

For each event in the process, there will be a key that allows you to set the account to be used for that event. Transaction/event keys can be added and changed, but this would be extremely rare, and we definitely do not recommend the practice. It is best to work with the existing keys and treat them as if they are unchangeable. Typical examples are BSX, PRD, and WRX.

Once the terminology is understood, the real challenge begins. The process itself can appear to be a black box, but in fact depends on three basic pieces of information:

▶ What is happening?
▶ Where is it happening?
▶ What is it happening to?

The combination of these three facts controls which account is to be updated. If the same thing is happening in the same place to the same type of material, the account used will be the same, but if any of these differ the account used can be different. The three elements of the process can be thought of as follows:

▶ The "what is happening" could be a posting to the GR/IR Clearing account following the posting of an invoice relating to an item that has been received. This is the transaction/event key selected by the system that suits the action aking place.

▶ The "where is it happening" affects the account to be used if you have decided to have different valuation areas (i.e., plants) treated differently.

▶ The "what is it happening to" uses the valuation class to determine which account is to be updated.

The transaction/event key is derived from the SAP transaction. The valuation area (or valuation area group if used) is derived from the plant, and the valuation class is derived from the material.

During configuration, you now have to set up the correct G/L account number for each of the combinations of these three variables. Any combination that you don't use can be left as long as you are sure that this situation will never arise.

Figure 4.8 shows the first page of the list of **transaction/event keys** shown when you select **Account assignment** from the first screen of the automatic account-determination configuration transaction.

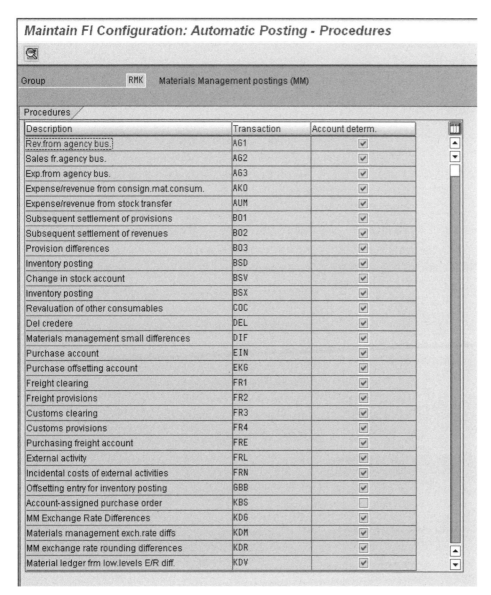

Figure 4.8 Transaction/Event Keys

To view or maintain the entries of a key:

▶ Double-click on the transaction/event key line.

▶ The system will ask you to enter the chart of accounts (COA) that you wish to work with. This only happens the first time you select a key; subsequently the system remembers the COA used previously.

▶ The next screen displayed will vary depending on how that key has been set up. Each key has associated "rules," and these determine how many variables can be used to affect the account used.

▶ To view or maintain the rules, you click on the **Rules** function box on the accounts screen, as shown in Figure 4.9.

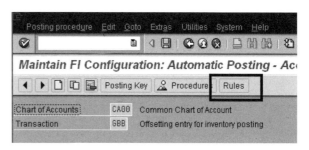

Figure 4.9 Rules Function Box

Up to four rules can be flagged, and the number of flags available is linked directly to the **transaction/event key**. The standard settings of these flags are often correct, but you may have to change the settings for some keys.

> **Note:** Changing the rule flag on a transaction/event key will cause all entries to be removed from the configuration of that key. Only change the flags if you are sure that you want this to happen.

The four keys are as follows (see Figure 4.10):

▶ **Debit/Credit**—With this flag set off you will only have one field for the account number and so debits and credits will be posted to the same account. If you set this flag on you will have the ability to set a different account number for each. postings

▶ **General modification**—This controls the extra variable called the account modifier. This field is not relevant to invoice verification; it is used to indicate the movement type that was used.

▶ **Valuation modif.**—This is the flag that controls the variable valuation area group (although you would never guess this by the name!). Set this off, and all postings to this event key will use the same account even if different plants are involved. Set it on and you can specify different accounts for each valuation area group that you have configured.

▶ **Valuation class**—Set this on if you want the account to depend on the valuation class of the material involved.

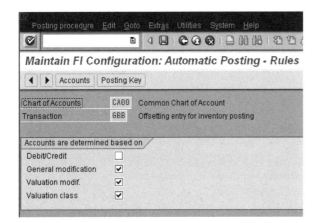

Figure 4.10 The Four Rules Available on Each Transaction/Event Key

Some keys will have all rules switched off. These are rules that involve postings where the account is not determined by the plant or material involved and where the same account is used for debit and credit postings.

One such key is the WRX transaction/event key; this is used for postings to the GR/IR Clearing account. In this case, the main use of a clearing account is to collect all postings in the same account so they can be cleared against each other. Thus, it is not normal to have multiple accounts.

Figure 4.11 shows the **Maintain FI Configuration: Automatic Posting—Accounts** screen of the WRX key where the only setting available is the G/L account number to be used.

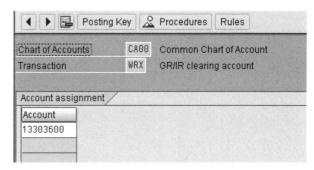

Figure 4.11 GR/IR Clearing Account Configuration Showing Only an Account-Number Entry

Other keys may have all four flags set on. This will enable a different account to be specified for each scenario in a large combination of scenarios. This is normally used only for materials-management-type postings such as goods issues, where the movement type (via the account modifier), the plant (via the valuation area/group), and the material (via the valuation class) all have an influence on the account used. The fourth flag sets on the option of separate debit and credit accounts.

There is no easy way to ensure that you process each transaction/event key. You have to configure each one that is relevant to your implementation, and there are no safe short cuts to this process. It is much better to configure a key that may not ever be used than to miss one and find out during use that this has been missed.

The other two main options in account determination, **Simulation,** and **G/L accounts,** are very useful for checking that the account configuration is complete and correct.

Simulation

This function is also available within account determination, where it is used to simulate postings in order to verify which accounts will be used and to help determine if everything has been configured correctly. Figure 4.12 shows the function box to select to enter the simulation mode.

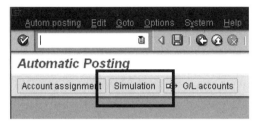

Figure 4.12 Simulation Function Box

The first time you use simulation, check the settings before you start. Select **Options** from the menu, and make the following settings for each of the three options, given below:

▶ Application area: This should be set to **Simulation** for invoice-verification transactions.

▶ Input mode: This should ideally be set to **Input of Valuation Class** so that you do not have to specify a material number. You may wish to set to **Input of Material Number** if you prefer to specify a material number instead, but this does rely on that material number existing with an accounting view.

▶ Account check: This should be set to **Check of Referenced G/L Accounts** unless you have not yet set up the general-ledger account master data.

When the simulation screen appears, enter the **Plant** (so that the system can determine the valuation area/group), the **Material** (or valuation class) and then select the scenario you wish to simulate (so that the system can determine the transaction/event keys that apply). Figure 4.13 shows the simulation-screen selection options.

The results of the simulation will be displayed. The header will show the organization details, and the system will have determined the company code, chart of accounts, valuation area, and valuation area group, all from the plant you specified.

Each potential posting will be displayed, but this does not mean that every posting will occur. The system is just

showing every posting that is possible, depending on the circumstances involved (standard price or MAP, material-specified or not relevant, etc.).

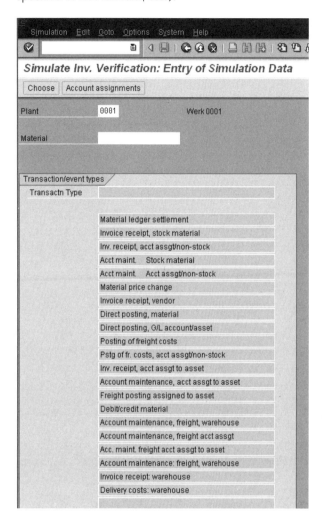

Figure 4.13 Simulation Selection Screen

Each G/L account that has been determined will be displayed. If the G/L account field shows—**Missing** this does not necessarily mean that anything is wrong. It just means that if that particular combination of events occurs, no account could be determined. It may well be that this combination of events will never happen in your implementation, and so missing entries are not always errors.

The **AM** field shows the account modifier if applicable. For almost all invoice-verification simulations, this will show -**e**-, meaning that no modifier applies. Figure 4.14 shows a sample simulation.

Use the simulation whenever you need to check the settings and don't necessarily want to create purchase orders, goods receipts, and invoice-verification postings.

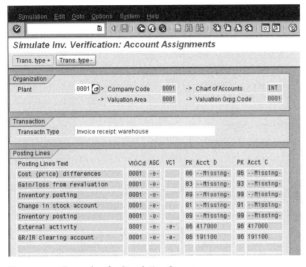

Figure 4.14 Example of a Simulation Screen

The G/L Accounts Function

This is, in my opinion, a hidden gem of a function. It will display all of the accounts that will be posted to via automatic account determination, and it also will show under what circumstances those accounts are posted to. It can be run at any stage and provides a report designed to help the accounts department determine if the correct accounts are being used.

You merely enter the company code or valuation area (plant) and the system will list the accounts used. Figure 4.15 shows where the function can be triggered. Figure 4.16 shows an example of a result.

Figure 4.15 G/L Accounts Function Box

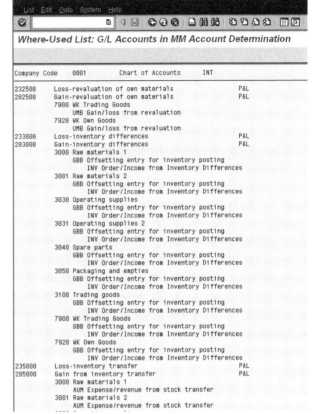

Figure 4.16 Sample Result

4.5 Incoming Invoice

This section of the configuration menu controls the settings that affect the posting of an invoice within the invoice-verification transaction. The only exception is the control of the blocking of invoices for payment. A configuration for this is contained in a separate section of the menu. Figure 4.17 shows the contents of the **Incoming Invoice** section of the configuration menu.

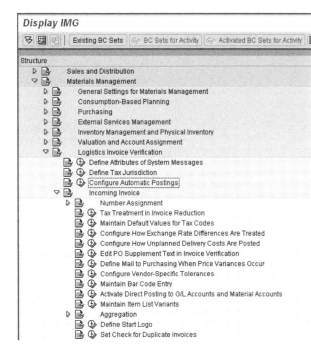

Figure 4.17 Incoming Invoice Configuration Sub-Menu

Number Assignment

There are two separate sections to this function:

▶ **Maintain Number Assignments for Accounting Documents**

This section includes the number assignments and document types for all accounting documents (RE and RN being the two main Invoice document types). Within this transaction, you can allocate number ranges and configure document types. It is advisable to retain and use the standard document types and number ranges provided by the system.

▶ **Maintain Number Assignment for Logistics Documents**

This is broken down to two further options:

▷ **Transaction—Assign Number Range,** in which the internal document types are linked to a number range ID. Here, too, the recommendation is to leave these as standard.

▷ **Maintain Number Range Intervals for Invoice Documents**, which allows you to manage the number ranges (although this can also be maintained in the **Maintain Number Assignments for Accounting Documents** option).

Although the **Maintain Number Assignments for Accounting Documents**. Configuration option appears to only deal with number ranges, it also allows you to configure the document types. There are two main document types used in invoice verification. These are:

▶ RE

▶ RN

The difference between the two main document types is the way that cash discounts (for prompt payment) are handled.

If you choose to use **RN** (net) then any discounts that are relevant to the payment terms associated to the invoice will be assumed to be applicable, and the total payment to the vendor will be reduced by the discount due.

Choosing **RN** (the more commonly used document type) will post the full value as due to the vendor, and the discounts will be calculated as part of the payment run. They will be applied only if they are due according to the payment terms and the actual payment date. Figure 4.18 shows the **RN** document type and the flag that controls the calculation.

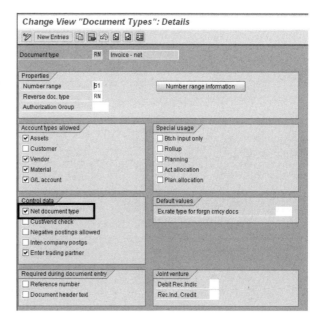

Figure 4.18 RN Document Type and Related Flag

Tax Treatment in Invoice Reduction

This configuration option determines where the tax correction is applied when invoice reduction is involved. Refer to Section 2.5 for details of this functionality.

You can post the tax correction on the original document; that is, you can have the correct tax posted against the erroneous invoice with no tax in the credit note.

Alternatively, you can have the incorrect tax value posted in the original document, to match the incorrect invoice value. In the latter case, a correction tax can be posted in the complaint document, which is the automatic credit note created during invoice reduction.

There is no major advantage to doing this one way over the other, but if you normally have the system calculate taxes automatically it is often better to use the tax correction in the original document setting. The setting can be different for each company code used. Figure 4.19 shows the configuration screen.

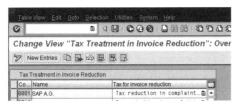

Figure 4.19 Tax Treatment in Invoice Reduction Screen

Maintain Default Values for Tax Codes

This configuration option controls which tax code is proposed by the system when an invoice is posted. It also controls which tax code is proposed by the system when unplanned delivery costs are posted. Figure 4.20 shows the configuration screen used to set the default tax codes.

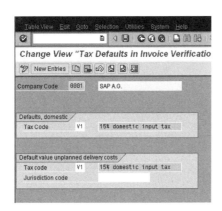

Figure 4.20 Default Tax Code Setting

Configure How Exchange- Rate Differences are Treated

Two main options are available from which to choose:

▶ You can treat exchange-rate differences as such
▶ You can treat them the same as any other price variance

If you choose to treat them as exchange rate differences, you have two different ways to control exactly how the difference is calculated. These are:

▶ One option will determine the difference between the exchange rate at the time of goods receipt and the exchange rate at the time of invoice verification.
▶ The other option determines the difference between the exchange rate at the time of invoice verification and an assumed or budget exchange rate.

You specify in the configuration settings which exchange rate stored on the exchange rate table is to be used in the calculation (in the **ERT** field). Figure 4.21 shows the configuration screen.

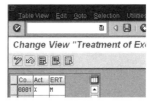

Figure 4.21 Exchange Rate Configuration Screen

Configure How Unplanned Delivery Costs are Posted

When you add unplanned delivery costs to an invoice during invoice verification (see Section 2.2) you can handle these in two different ways. The system can either spread the costs among the items on the invoice, or it can create a separate line on the invoice and post the costs to that line.

The latter option does not pass the costs to the materials, so choose this option if you want that result. The setting is controlled by company code. Figure 4.22 shows the configuration screen.

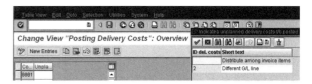

Figure 4.22 Posting Delivery Costs Configuration Screen

Edit PO Supplement Text in Invoice Verification

Within this option, you can specify if you want notifiable texts to be displayed during invoice verification and, if so, which texts should trigger the message. See Chapter 2 for details of the functionality. In short, you need to:

1. Select the **Order text general** option to specify the company codes that are relevant to this option.

2. Select the **Notifiable order text types** to specify which purchase-order header texts should trigger the message in invoice verification. To do this, you need to add a new entry for the required company code and then double-click the company code and choose the header text types from the options displayed.

Figure 4.23 shows the two main options to be selected.

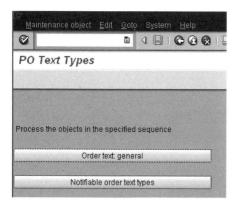

Figure 4.23 Two Main Options to Control Notifiable Texts

Figure 4.24 shows an example of the notifiable texts.

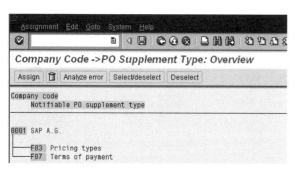

Figure 4.24 Notifiable Texts Screen

Define Mail to Purchasing When Price Variances Occur

This configuration setting can be used to ensure that a message is sent to a user when an invoice price variance occurs. This is sent as an email or SAPmail message depending on how your technical team has set up this kind of communication.

The user informed would normally be the buyer or the person who raised the purchase order. Within this configuration step, you merely decide if a message should be sent (the choice controlled by a flag for each company code).

In the message-determination configuration, you decide how the system determines who to send the message to and also what format the message takes.

Configure Vendor-Specific Tolerances

Even though this is called "vendor-specific," you don't actually specify a vendor in the configuration. You specify a tolerance group, and the vendor master record also contains a tolerance group. In effect, these are vendor-tolerance group tolerances. There are two main options:

▶ A simple tolerance that will post any differences for this group of vendors to a "small differences account" if the differences are within the tolerances specified (percentage and/or value and with a negative and/or positive difference)

▶ An automatic invoice reduction tolerance that will cause an automatic credit note to be raised for the difference, if it is within the tolerances set. See Section 2.5 for an explanation of invoice reduction.

Set the check-limit flag if you want that specific tolerance to be considered, and enter the tolerance percentage and/or value you want to apply. These settings are controlled by company code and tolerance group. See Figure 4.25 for a sample tolerance configuration.

Maintain Bar-Code Entry

This configuration controls the ability to store a bar code along with the invoice details. You create a new entry for each company code for which you wish to capture bar codes and enter document types that are relevant for bar-code storage. This will trigger an additional window in the invoice-verification transaction MIRO where you can input the bar code.

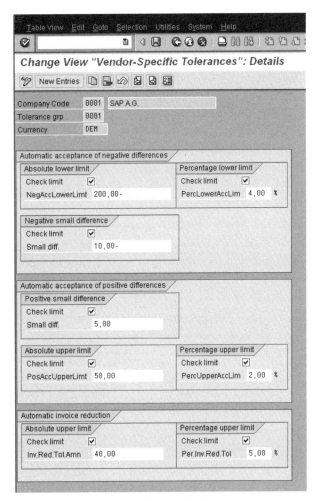

Figure 4.25 Vendor-Specific Tolerance Settings

Activate Direct Posting to G/L Accounts and Material Account

With this configuration option, you can switch on the ability to enter additional lines on the invoice at invoice verification entry, even if the extra line is not contained on the purchase order. Simply flag the required option or options, described below:

▶ The **Dir.posting to G/L acct = active** option allows the user to add additional lines to the invoice posting if they refer to a general ledger account

▶ The **Dir. Posting to matl = active** option allows the user to add additional lines to the invoice posting if they refer to material master records

Leave both flags set off if the invoice-verification function is only to be used for entries that relate to purchase-order lines. If you want your entry clerks to be able to add addi-

tional lines to an invoice within MIRO, then switch the appropriate flag or flags on.

Maintain Item-List Variants

In this option, you specify the layout of the line display in the Invoice-Verification main screen. In effect, you are maintaining a type of screen variant with each field selectable. If you wish to change anything, it is best to leave the existing standard layouts as they are and create copies.

Aggregation

The aggregation function in Invoice-Verification controls what aggregation of line items occurs. If the invoice total matches the total value of all of the purchase orders keyed against the invoice, the match can be made.

The configuration controls the way that the items can be aggregated. The first step **Maintain Variants for Aggregation List** acts in the same way as the **Maintain Item List Variants** does, and the screens look identical (although different programs are used).

The second step—**Preset Aggregation Criteria**—is where the controls are entered against the aggregation variant that the settings relate to. You specify the elements of the purchase orders to be aggregated, such as delivery note, material, etc. The detail-configuration screen is shown in Figure 4.26.

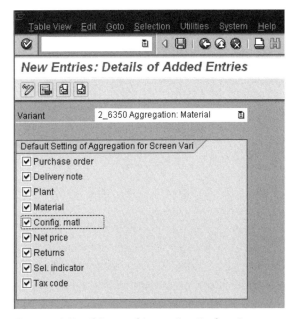

Figure 4.26 Detail Screen of Aggregation Configuration

Define Start Logo

Although this merely allows you to display a logo on the invoice-verification screen, it is far more useful than it at first appears.

Many implementations involve multiple company codes. If you set a different logo for each company, this could prevent erroneous entries, and the user would be able to spot the difference easily if the wrong company code was specified. Without this logo, it is not easy to see which company code has been defaulted.

You merely flag the company code to switch on the display within MIRO and specify the URL where the logo is stored, normally in a directory on your network.

Set Check for Duplicate Invoices

This configuration controls the check for duplicate entries that is applied to the reference-document number entered at the time of invoice entry. This reference field is normally used to capture the vendor's invoice number. With the check activated, the user will receive a message if the same reference number has already been used on another invoice, because this could indicate that the invoice has already been posted.

You need to indicate whether this check should take place and, if so, what check should be carried out. You achieve this by setting the three flags on the relevant company code line.

The first flag, **Check co. code,** should be set on if you want the system to check for the same reference number within the same company code. Set the flag off if you want to check for duplicates across all company codes.

The second flag, **Check reference,** controls whether the check should take place at all. Leave this off if you do not want to check for duplicates. This could be necessary if you are not using the reference field for the vendor's invoice number and as a result duplicates will often occur.

The final flag, **Check inv. Date** should be set on if you want to check for duplicate entries on the same date. With this flag set off, duplicates will be allowed as long as they have a different invoice date. This setting could be useful if a vendor sends in invoices with the same reference number, but on different dates.

4.6 Document Parking

You only need to configure these settings if you want to block parked invoices from further processing, depending on the value of the invoice.

This is a rarely used function. If you do want to use this functionality, the configuration step should only be completed by an experienced workflow consultant. The definition of the release criteria, however, is not complicated. The configuration controls those invoices that are parked. It prevents them from being fully posted until they have been released by an authorized user.

The **Define Release Criteria** step allows you to set up an authorization process. You specify the company code that is to be controlled and specify the person or function that is to be responsible for the release of the document. You can have many entries with different value levels. If the document has a value below the limit, it is not blocked. If it is above this limit, then it is blocked for posting and—depending on the value—it will be allocated to a specified user. Figure 4.27 shows the **Define Release Criteria** configuration screen.

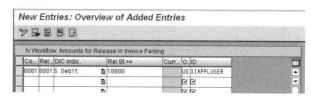

Figure 4.27 Define Release Criteria Configuration Screen

4.7 Invoice Block

This section of the configuration is where you will set up the payment blocks and how they are used. Payment blocks are needed to prevent invoices from being paid due to mismatches or to block matched invoices for payment in disputes and other special situations.

The main tolerances are controlled here. Remember that invoice tolerances don't stop the invoice from being posted; they merely indicate whether the payment block should be set. If the payment block is applied to an invoice, it will behave exactly like an invoice that has not been blocked, but the payment run will not automatically pay the vendor. All financial postings and all other updates still take place even though there is a mismatch.

Determine Payment Block

All that you need to do in this step is to configure any additional payment blocks that you need. These would be manual blocks that the user could enter during invoice verification. You can only change the descriptions of the main blocks, as no other settings are controlled here. Normally, you do not need to do anything in this step.

Set Tolerance Limits

This is a very important step and should be carried out with the full involvement of the financial department. This configuration will control the situations where an exact match cannot be determined. The difference between the amount due to the vendor and the value of the invoice can be allowed, and so can result in over-payments. It is therefore vital that the tolerances are fully agreed upon by all interested parties before invoices are posted for the first time.

The settings will be used to block invoices that exceed the set tolerances and prevent the automatic payment. There are no recommended tolerance levels. The levels used depend on many different factors, the most important of which is the actual cost of investigating discrepancies.

If the cost of investigating a mismatch is very low, then you can set your tolerances to be reasonably strict. If the cost of investigating mismatches is high, then you should consider being slightly more lenient.

For example, the time involved can be significant if you take into consideration the time taken to post the invoice initially (which will be longer because of the mismatch), the time taken to pass on the invoice for investigation, the actual time during the investigation (including telephone calls and letters etc.), plus the time taken to finally clear the mismatch.

Let's assume for this example that the cost is in the region of €50. If you have set the tolerance value to block invoices where the vendor has overcharged you by more than €10, then you will effectively spend €50 to regain €10. Of course, if the vendor was to find out that you have a tolerance of €50, and they were not thoroughly honest, they could ensure that they always overcharged by €49. Therefore, you have to choose sensible levels that are low enough to trap overcharges but not so low

that you are spending more on matching than the over-charges you are trapping.

If you are setting up a new company code in your development system, copying the tolerances shown in Figure 4.28 from Company Code 0001 will at least enable you to raise invoices. You can then adjust the settings as you learn the precise tolerances you require.

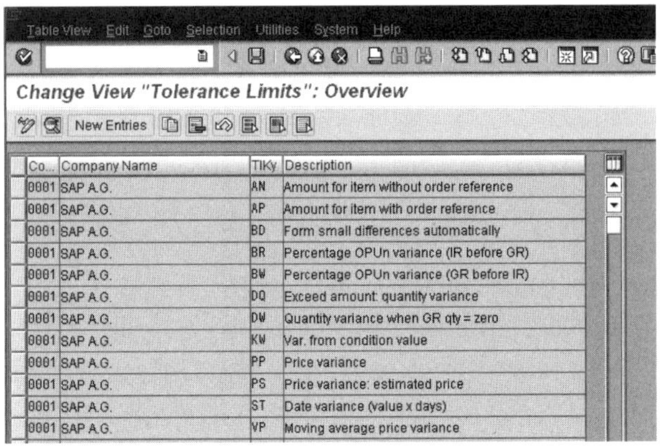

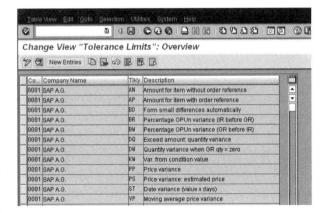

Figure 4.28 Basic Set of Tolerances

The main tolerances all have upper and lower limits for percentage and value. The value is in the default currency of the company code. You also have flags that indicate that the tolerance should be checked. Figure 4.29 shows a typical tolerance with all of the settings available.

Figure 4.29 Typical Invoice Tolerance Screen

The following tolerances are the most common:
- **AN** (Amount for item without order reference): This tolerance is used when a line has been added to the invoice that does not reference a purchase order (or similar document). Use this tolerance to block

invoices with manual entries. The tolerance limit is normally quite high because your own clerks have entered this data.

▶ **AP** (Amount for item with order reference): This tolerance is used if you wish to block invoice ines that exceed a certain value even if they fully match against a referenced document. This is normally set very high and is often seen as a block that is used as a comfort factor, so that large invoice values can be checked. Often this tolerance value is increased after a short period when it becaomes clear that the system is operating correctly and capturing erroneous invoices automatically.

▶ **BD** (Form small differences automatically): Use extreme caution with this tolerance. It should be set very low indeed, for instance €0.05 or less. It is designed to manage rounding errors (typically caused by tax calculations). It is unique in that it does not set the blocking flag on the invoice but merely allows a tolerance when the mathematical check is carried out to ensure that the invoice value equates to the data entered.

▶ **BR** and **BW** (Percentage OPUn variance with IR before GR and Percentage OPUn variance with GR before IR): This is a tolerance that checks the order price unit variances. An example of the order price unit is where you may purchase one barrel of a fluid and the price is €50 a barrel and the barrel is to contain 50 liters. If the receipt is for one barrel, but there are only 40 liters in the barrel, then the order price has varied. This tolerance allows the vendor some leeway when it comes to invoices for items that fall onto this category where the contents can vary under normal circumstances.

▶ **DQ** (Exceed amount: quantity variance): This tolerance controls quantity variances. If you purchase bulk materials, the actual quantities can vary and so you may wish to allow some tolerance on invoices. If you only purchase items that have specific quantities, you may wish to set this tolerance to zero. Even though this is a quantity variance, the system takes the value of the item into consideration. In this way, a small quantity discrepancy on an expensive item may be blocked, but a larger discrepancy on a lower priced item may be allowed.

▶ **DW** (Quantity variance when GR qty = zero): The system will use the purchase order price to calculate the value of the item, as opposed to the goods-receipt value used in the previous tolerance. If you don't maintain this tolerance for your company code, the system will block an invoice for which no goods receipt has been posted. If you want to allow the posting of such an invoice, set the tolerance limits for this tolerance to **Do not check**.

▶ **KW** (Var. from condition value): This tolerance focuses on the planned delivery costs and will block an invoice if the invoiced planned delivery cost varies from the value stored on the condition type used on the conditions on the purchase order.

▶ **LA** (Amount of blanket purchase order): The system will check the total invoiced value for the blanket purchase order plus this invoice against the value limits specified in the order. The tolerances will dictate if the invoice should be blocked.

▶ **LD** (Blanket purchase order time limit exceeded): This compares the invoice date against the allowed invoice interval on the purchase order and blocks the invoice if the tolerance has been exceeded.

▶ **PP** (Price variance): This can be set to allow small price variances. The lower limit and percentage would appear to be unnecessary, so why would you want to block an invoice for payment simply because the vendor has undercharged you? The answer is that you probably wouldn't, but if the difference is high then perhaps there has been a keying error or a vendor error, and so it would be worth verifying the facts before making the payment. I would recommend setting a relatively high lower tolerance for underpayments.

▶ **PS** (Price variance: estimated price): This is another hidden gem that is often overlooked even though it can be very useful. There are often certain vendors or certain purchase orders where the price is almost always wrong because you do not always know when the purchase order is raised. There may be further actions after ordering that affect the price, for instance. If this is the case, you can flag the price as an estimated price in the purchase order condition control tab (as seen in Figure 4.30). This will ensure that the estimated price tolerance is checked instead

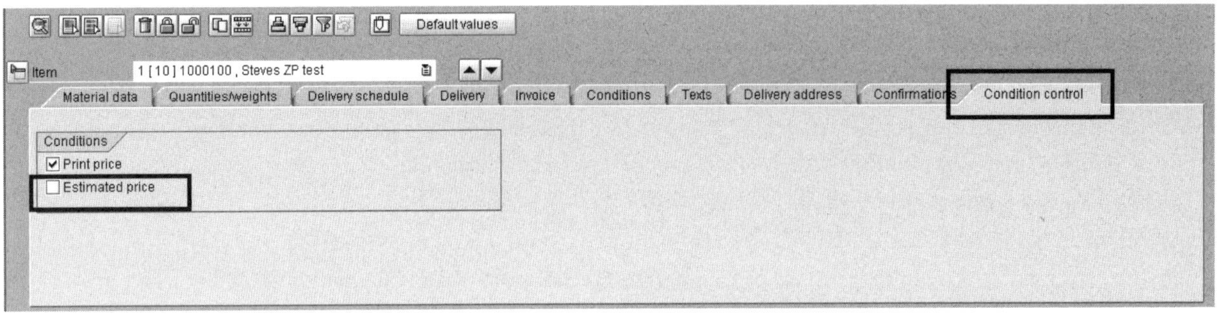

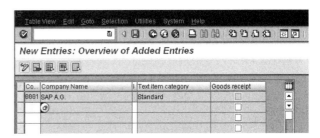

Figure 4.30 Estimated Price Flag

of the normal price-variance tolerance. This flag is ideal in situations where you have variable prices but there is an element of trust with the vendor used.

▶ **ST** (Date variance—value X days): This tolerance is actually a number of days multiplied by the invoice value. It is used to prevent the early payment to a vendor when it has delivered the goods early and sent the invoice before the delivery date has been reached. Multiplying the value by the number of days early (invoice date compared to the delivery date on the purchase order) gives the figure that is checked against the tolerance. This means that an item 100 days early valued at €10 will be treated the same as an item one day early with a value of €1,000.

▶ **VP** (Moving average price variance): This tolerance does not affect the invoice block, but instead is used to warn the user that the invoice posting will affect the MAP by an amount that exceeds the tolerance. This is an important setting, because if an invoice price is different from the MAP it will alter that MAP, even if the invoice is blocked for payment. This would normally trigger a warning message (i.e. the user can continue) but the message can be set to an error if you want to prevent the corruption of the MAP, a topic covered in Chapter 3.

Item Amount Check

This is not actually a tolerance, but rather a setting that will indicate to the system if the item value should be checked against the **AP** and **AN** tolerances described above.

You can first indicate if the check should be carried out, using the **Activate Amount Check** configuration. You merely flag the company codes that you want to use

for the check. In the **Set Item Amount Check** you specify the type of order line to be checked.

One use for this setting is to block all items that have the GR (Goods Receipt) flag set off. With this flag set off, there is no three-way matching because the flag indicates whether a goods receipt is necessary. Without a goods receipt, there is nothing to check at the invoice stage relating to quantity.

So, in this case you can set the item amount check to be triggered if the item has the GR flag set off. You can also specify the item category if required, so that you can carry out the tolerance check on special purchase orders such as sub-contract, etc.

Figure 4.31 shows an example of a setting in which the system will check all purchase order lines where the GR flag has been set off (in this case for all purchase orders with a standard item category).

Figure 4.31 Set Item Amount Check Screen

Stochastic Blocks

A stochastic block is effectively a random block. It is designed to block a portion of invoices that normally would not have been blocked. It is also designed to be used as a type of spot check. It can be quite scary to have all invoices automatically paid if they match. This is especially true when SAP is being used for the first time in a company. This check can be used to increase confidence in the automatic matching process. The invoices blocked in this way can be selected when using the MRBR transaction, so that they can be subject to a second manual check. Figure 4.32 shows the flag that can be set on MRBR to show invoices that have been stochastically blocked.

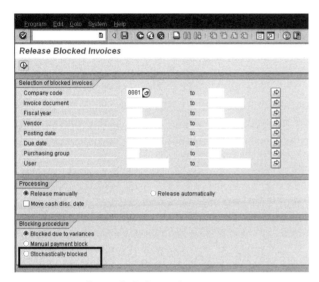

Figure 4.32 Stochastic Block Flag on the MRBR Transaction

The first step is to use the **Activate Stochastic Block** function to flag the company codes that you want to take part in the check. The second step is to use the **Set Stochastic Block** function to set the parameters. There are two parameters: the **Threshold value** and the **Percentage**. The parameters work as follows.

Set the **Percentage** as the percentage of invoices that you want to be randomly blocked. Every invoice equal to, or over the **Threshold value** will be considered to be relevant, and the specified percentage of these invoices will be blocked. Invoices below this value will still be considered by the stochastic check, but as the value reduces so does the chance of them being stochastically blocked.

In this manner an invoice with a value of half of the threshold is half as likely to be blocked as an invoice that is equal to or greater than the threshold value. So the threshold is not value above which the invoices will be stochastically blocked. It is, rather, a ceiling for the percentage above which the percentage likelihood of the invoice being blocked stays the same, but below which the likelihood decreases proportionately.

4.8 Clearing-Account Maintenance

This configuration step simply controls the number ranges that relate to the clearing accounts for GR/IR, freight, and customs postings.

4.9 Invoice Verification in Background

This configuration step allows you to set a flag that will set a different status on the invoice if it has been verified in the background. Remember to keep the following in mind:

▶ Set the flag on if you want the matched invoices to have the status set so that they can be identified as being correct but not complete.

▶ Set the flag set off if you want invoices posted in the background will appear as completed and so will appear identical to those manually posted.

4.10 Electronic Data Interchange

If you accept invoices via Electronic Data Interchange (EDI), then you can use these settings to convert the data on the EDI record to the correct data used in your system. Tax codes and company codes can be converted. The third step allows you to make various settings that indicate how the invoice data should be processed. These settings indicate which invoice document type should be used, whether the documents should be parked or fully posted, and which checks should be carried out. Figure 4.33 (see next page) shows the settings that can be made in the third step, **Enter Program Parameters**.

4.11 Message Determination

This step controls the output, printing, emails, etc. of any messages or documents. This is the standard SAP method of using the condition technique to control the output and is not covered here.

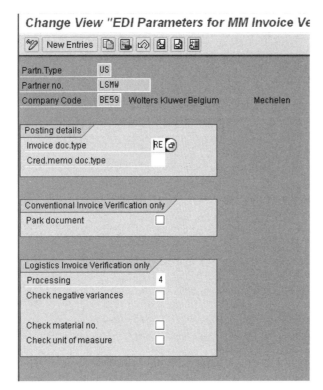

Figure 4.33 Available Program Parameters

4.12   Define Document Life

In this step, you define the number of days that a fully processed invoice should remain in the system before it is considered by the archiving run.

4.13   Authorization Management.

In this step, your authorization consultant can manage the authorization profiles and maintain the authorizations, but there is a step that can be used to control the limits of groups of users. This is controlled by the use of tolerance groups. If you assign users to tolerance groups, you can then limit these groups by company code. The limits you can control are:

▶ The total value per document
▶ The value per open account item
▶ The maximum cash discount that can be used
▶ A set of permitted payment differences

4.14   Maintain Customer Exits and Business Add-Ins

In this step, your technical team can manage any user exits that are required.

4.15   Logistics Invoice Verification: Index

This is not actually a configuration step. It provides instructions on how to use the index on the invoice-verification documents. Unless you have a very small quantity of invoices, switching on this index will speed up bulk processing and reports. There will be additional overhead on the creation of new documents (as the index is maintained on line), but this overhead should almost be invisible.

4.16   Summary

In this chapter, the configuration of invoice verification was discussed. Remember that the SAP help available within configuration will also help explain the options available.

My own style of configuration is to use the options available to the full, and this often results in fewer user exits and or modifications.

I firmly believe that the standard SAP invoice-verification functionality is so rich (especially with the use of the many configuration options) that you should not have to employ any user-exits or modifications. If you believe that you do need to use these, then please make sure that you are not changing the system to match the business, when a change to the business may, in the long run, lead to a better system altogether.

Index

ISBN   1-59229-083-3

ISBN13   978-1-59229-083-3

1st edition

© 2006 by Galileo Press GmbH

SAP PRESS is an imprint of Galileo Press,

Boston (MA), USA

Bonn, Germany

Editor Jawahara Saidullah
Copy Editor/Proofreader John Parker
Cover Design Vera Brauner
Printed in Germany